MEMORY MEADOWS

GRANT MACEWAN

MEMORY MEADOWS

TIMELESS HORSE STORIES

GREYSTONE BOOKS

Douglas & McIntyre Publishing Group
Vancouver/Toronto/New York

Copyright © 1976 by Grant MacEwan
First Greystone edition 1997

03 04 05 06 07   5 4 3 2

This book was originally published by Western Producer
Prairie Books, a publishing venture owned by Saskatchewan
Wheat Pool.

Greystone Books
A division of Douglas & McIntyre Ltd.
2323 Quebec Street, Suite 201
Vancouver, British Columbia
Canada V5T 4S7
www.greystonebooks.com

National Library of Canada Cataloguing in Publication Data
MacEwan, Grant, 1902–2000
    Memory meadows

    ISBN 1-55054-568-X

    1. Horses—Anecdotes. 2. Horses—Canada—History. I. Title.
SF301.M24 1997   636.1′00971   C96-910840-0

Cover design by Peter Cocking
Cover photo © Richard Cummins/CORBIS/MAGMA
Printed and bound in Canada by Transcontinental
Printed on acid-free paper
Distributed in the U.S. by Publishers Group West

We gratefully acknowledge the financial support of the Canada
Council for the Arts, the British Columbia Arts Council, and the
Government of Canada through the Book Publishing Industry
Development Program (BPIDP) for our publishing activities.

For Fiona and Lynwyn
and all other Canadians young and old
who like stories about real horses.

Contents

CONTENTS

Preface

If today's horses were aware of their multimillion-year history on this North American soil, they would be the proudest of all contemporary creatures. The long, slow evolutionary rise from a small form no bigger than a fox terrier to something of modern horse proportions is permanently recorded on "the pages of the rocks" and will bear study.

The intervening aeons of time were not without serious reverses that threatened the survival of the race. As fossil remains show, the wild North American horses became extremely numerous and remained so until struck by a destructive force of unproven character. It is not clear whether it was disease, an increase in natural enemies, a severe shift in climate, or an upheaval in natural balances due to the appearance of a new race. We may never know, but whatever it was, it left the continent completely horseless. The species might have died out altogether if it had not been for earlier migrations of North American horse stock to Asia, and thence to other parts of the world, by way of Bering Strait. At one time, accumulations of glacial ice resulted in a drop in ocean levels and a land bridge between the two continents, making migration possible.

Horses must have multiplied on the Asian grasslands and been domesticated there. It is easy to imagine what would happen next; horses for riding and driving would spread to Europe, North Africa, and Arabia, then improved horses to Spain and back to North America with the Spaniards who followed Columbus.

Imported strains gave rise to Indian horses, the seminative mustangs, horses for agriculture, for war, for freighting, ranching, police work, construction in a thousand forms, and recreation. Horses became an integral and crucial work force on pioneer farms, and to forget the early human debt to them would represent a grave injustice. Too often the horse was overworked and underfed, and frequently the faithful brute's life was terminated the day after its usefulness ended. There were, of course, some horsemen who tried to pay a humane debt by granting old horses a spell of ease and affectionate care.

Perhaps there should be more monuments to the memory of all work stock in the years before mechanical power. Certainly we should record with gratitude the role of the horse before it was displaced by tractor power; these memories ought to be kept alive.

It is unquestionable that there were horses possessing rare individuality in both temperament and performance—just as there were humans with important individual differences; some of these animals performed a heroic sort of service. Their stories should not be lost. It was in the hope of paying a tribute to all of mankind's faithful equine friends and conferring a special accolade on a few with rare performance records that led to the preparation and publication of this book, *Memory Meadows*.

Published initially in 1976, the book was well received and went through four printings. Now, as the book is being prepared for its fifth printing, the author desires to thank Western Producer Prairie Books for the opportunity of expanding it slightly through the addition of a few new chapters.

1

Fireaway

Wonder Horse of the Frontier

As traders and travelers in the early West remembered the stallion, Fireaway, "he had everything." He had enough speed to overtake a herd of fleeing buffalo or leave native horses far behind in a Red River race, enough stamina to carry a hunter all day, and enough beauty and character to fill horse thieves with the urge to steal him. "What a horse!" men exclaimed. He was the unbeatable, unforgettable, unbelievable, and for more than thirty years after his disappearance from prairie scenes, sons and daughters were still winning attention and commanding premium prices.

Very properly, Fireaway could claim a long list of firsts. Beyond any question, he was the first horse of his breed — Norfolk Trotter or Hackney — to be brought to Canadian soil, first horse of any improved breed to be brought to the new West, first to materially change the quality of the native horse stock. Altogether, this imported horse became a legend on the frontier. Most citizens in the buffalo country had never heard of Pegasus, the winged horse of Greek mythology, but they were familiar with this Wonder Horse of Red River, Fireaway the Marvelous, and were inspired.

True, the horse was brought to the West at a time in history when it would not be difficult for a good animal to make an impression and gain fame. The Selkirk settlers, Western Canada's first real farmers, began coming in 1812 and their needs were many and urgent.

Fortunately, the new land to which the courageous settlers were coming to make homes was not totally without horses. The country was without sheep and pigs and practically without cattle, but the prairie Indians held horses of a lowly strain tracing to introductions to the southern part of the North American continent by Spaniards about 300 years earlier. In the absence of any attempt to improve or even maintain quality in the existing stock, the animals were small and often undernourished and ill-shaped. In their favor, however, they were hardy, acclimatized and sure-footed. The Selkirk people were thankful to find and acquire some of them for work purposes.

But the British settlers longed for bigger horses — more like those in the home lands. Governor George Simpson of the Hudson's Bay Company believed that the provision of a good stallion would be of the greatest benefit to settlers. In 1830, he notified his business friends in London that about fifty of the native mares had been selected and gathered together at the new Experimental Farm in the settle-

2

ment for a breeding and improvement program. Obviously, a superior stallion was needed and company officials took the hint. The Deputy Governor wrote from London on February 25, 1831, to report that "a stallion of a proper breed" was being sent by ship to York Factory at the south end of Hudson Bay and gave it as his advice that the Experimental Farm in the Red River Colony would be "the best place at which to commence raising horses for the service."

This was good news and Simpson ordered preparations, at the same time confirming that the horse would be placed at the Experimental Farm "on the Assiniboine river, about four miles above the Forks."

The great horse arrived at York Factory late in the summer of 1831 when, after many weeks on the sailing ship, he still faced the bigger test, that of transportation by canoe or York boat over the water route of almost 700 miles from York Factory to Fort Garry. Carrying a grown and restless horse in a small craft on an upstream course on the treacherous rivers flowing into Hudson Bay had to be a most dangerous occupation and one likely to be extremely unpopular with voyageurs who had never before been required to share their canoe with a strange stallion. But apparently, the horse learned how to behave in a canoe, how to balance himself in rough water, and how to step into and out of the boat when portaging was necessary.

After more weeks of travel, Fireaway arrived at the Experimental Farm, safe and well. He was at once the center of attraction. He was of an imposing size, probably close to 16 hands in height. A red-roan in color, the animal was identified as a Norfolk Trotter, the strain or breed from which the better-known Hackney sprang. As an early test demonstrated,

Fireaway had unusual speed and that in itself was enough to ensure popularity.

Simpson was pleased to report by letter: "He is looked upon as one of the wonders of the world by the natives, many of whom have travelled great distances with no other object than to see him."

The breeding program proved successful and the progeny from Fireaway and the selected mares were the best buffalo runners and the best utility horses the settlers had used in this new land. The best compliment that could be paid to his popularity was in the several attempts to steal him. One of the plots detected was to whisk him away by night and take him south to the United States.

The popularity of Fireaway colts continued long after the horse was gone. Even in 1864, which was thirty-three years after Fireaway's importation, the Methodist missionary, John McDougall, traveled from Fort Edmonton to Fort Garry and felt rewarded at being able to buy a descendant of Fireaway for seventy dollars. The best horses for racing and chasing buffalo were still those that carried Fireaway blood.

Strangely enough, no record survived to tell exactly what happened to the famous horse. Numerous stories were told, one that he was stolen and taken southward, one that he was sold legitimately to go to the United States, one that he was so highly regarded that horsemen in England bought him and had him shipped back to his homeland. Perhaps he died at Red River, but nobody seems to be sure. But regardless of what happened to him in his last years, his importation was one of the best things undertaken to help the settlers in Western Canada's first farm colony.

2

The Wild Stallion

His Fight for Freedom

He was not very big and when he first came to public attention, he didn't even have a name; but with black coat glistening in the sunlight, a high carriage of head and a bold stride, he was both elegant and beautiful. Of course he was conscious of his position as leader of the untamed horse herd running in what is now western Saskatchewan and his spirit was that of a wild monarch, gay and proud and defiant.

Romantic tales were told about wild horses living like antelope and deer on prairie and intermountain grass — stallion fights for mastery of the herds, displays of courage in combat with enemies, bursts of unbelievable speed when pursued by Indians or white settlers seeking capture, and sundown appear-

5

ances with statuesque beauty in rimrock settings. Always, the stallion leader was the key figure in the story.

Here was mustang stock which had escaped from domestication some time after Spanish adventurers had brought horses back to the Western World. Having gained freedom, the animals were quick to adopt the wild ways of remote ancestors which had evolved and lived for millions of years on North American soil. It was like a return to native haunts.

Hunting wild horses became a pastime with adventure-loving men of the early West. It was a dangerous as well as an exciting occupation but there were various reasons for pursuing it. In a few instances, horses were hunted for their hides, and sometimes they were destroyed to reduce the spread of certain diseases like glanders. More often, they were pursued by Indians and settlers who needed horses for riding and farm work. Homesteaders in what became western Saskatchewan were well aware of a band of wild horses roaming the prairie country between Tramping Lake and Sounding Lake. This particular herd, headed by the defiant black stallion, was believed to trace to stock which had been abandoned after a notorious horse thief was driven from his dugout headquarters near Heart's Hill. Unclaimed, unbranded and unhampered, the horse herd lived on. But when settlers began to occupy the surrounding country, they looked covetously at the wild horses.

Jack Vallance, a young Scot who filed on a homestead about thirteen miles west of the town of Kerrobert in 1906 and represented the constituency of South Battleford in the Canadian House of Commons from 1925 to 1935, had a first-hand knowledge of those freedom-loving wild horses and the difficulties in capturing them. After driving a pair of oxen from Battleford on the first trip to the homestead, it was not surprising that he, like fellow settlers, looked enviously and hopefully at the wild horses. The need for more and better farm power was urgent but there was still another reason for the settlers' interest in capturing the wild stock. Homesteaders who were so fortunate as to have their own horses were losing an occasional animal to the wild herd. When a domestic horse was coaxed away to join the wild band and had tasted freedom, the chance of recovery was slight. Almost at once the escaped animal could become an outlaw, trying to forget forever about homestead stables and homestead toil.

When neighbors in that frontier community came together for social intercourse, conversation turned to the wild horses which had established their rendezvous in a swampy area near Balliol. "We've talked about it long enough," said one of Jack Vallance's neighbors. "Let's get at it." The idea was approved. A day was set. Plans were made and men became eager, like Thoroughbreds in a starting gate.

Of course, the wild horses would resist with all the speed and stamina they possessed. Capture would be extremely difficult. They could easily outrun the heavier work horses owned by the homesteaders and some special strategy would be necessary. More than that, those animals reared in the wilds would have a big advantage in being surefooted. While the domesticated animals would be likely to stumble, the wild ones would bound across rough ground without mishap or loss of speed. And, miraculously, the wild things would miss the treacherous badger holes as they galloped.

Everybody agreed: the wild horses would not be overtaken in a sprint. Nor would they be corralled.

The only hope was in a well-organized and prolonged effort with mounted men taking up the chase in relays. Only in this way could the homesteaders wear the wild horses down and exhaust them to the point of subjection. The drive would be started at an early morning hour and directed, as far as possible, along a circular route. In this way, new riders on fresh mounts could take up the chase at intervals of six or eight miles. And when any member of the wild band was overtaken in an exhausted state, it would be roped and its capture made secure.

The plan was well conceived, but when it got under way, it was soon evident that the drive was not one which would be completed in an hour or two. It might take more than a day. It did, and it became a test of men as well as horses. The wild things lacked nothing in cunning and courage, and in the first day of the attack, only one member of the mustang band was captured. The next day was better and two wild horses were taken. Quite obviously, the best ones would be the last to give up, probably the black stallion running constantly at the head of his band and a little bay mare that was never more than a few feet away from him. They would be the highest prizes in the hunt.

Men were quick to notice something unusual in the relationship between these two wild horses. The mare was always at the stallion's side. When the drive was being renewed after a pause, the stallion would whinny as if to give a signal and the bay mare would come to his side, touch her muzzle to his flank and remain close to him as they ran.

The drive wore on. Men as well as horses were becoming tired, but they were making some progress. After a lot of hard riding, only two wild horses remained to be captured, the proud stallion and his unfailing running mate, the little bay mare. "One more spurt," said the homesteader with whom Jack Vallance was riding, "and we'll have them." And one more spurt did accomplish the purpose; with odds overwhelmingly against them, the last wild pair, about ready to collapse, was taken into the pursuers' net.

Tired men were glad that the struggle had ended but they were not too tired to feel shocked in what they discovered about the little bay mare: She was totally blind. Only then was it clear why she always ran with her head at the stallion's flank. His eyes had served both of them. It was a magnificent example of devotion and loyalty in wild creatures. Homesteaders fell silent as they witnessed the climax and some would have been ready to release the gallant stallion and his little friend, forfeit the prizes they had worked so hard to win.

It did seem a shame to end the admirable relationship but pioneers needed horses most urgently. Necessity overruled sentiment and the captured horses were led away to enslavement.

It was considered impossible to make a fair distribution of the horses among those men who had participated in the drive and it was decided that the captives would be offered at auction. The little bay mare with the handicap of blindness was not worth much. There were those settlers who wished they had enough money to let them buy both the black stallion and the bay mare and allow them to live together on a grassy pasture. But the men on the new Saskatchewan soil could only dream of such a charitable gesture and the black stallion and his blind mate were led away to be separated forever.

There is no record of the mare's purchaser but the stallion was taken by Thorsen Brothers, of Luseland. Years passed and the story of the horse hunt was all but forgotten. Then, while traveling a prairie trail one summer day, Jack Vallance noticed a rather dejected little black gelding drawing an old buggy with five school children in it. There was something strikingly familiar about the horse and Vallance broke his journey to make some inquiries. He did not say so but one can imagine that tears came to his eyes when his hunch was confirmed; here, indeed, was the horse which had so proudly headed the wild band. As he turned away and gazed into space, Jack Vallance could see the heroic stallion leading his blind mate in that last desperate effort to escape with freedom. Then the man went back and touched the old horse, touched him tenderly, affectionately.

3

Prince

Leader of the Parade

Prince was Joe Humble's horse and both deserve to be remembered as distinguished pioneers in the Edmonton area.

Although totally blind in his later years, Joe Humble had many rich memories of frontier experiences as a horseman. He had been a homesteader, drayman and retail butcher, never without horses. Feelingly, he recalled the faithful animals serving him in those early years and with special affection he talked about Prince, the stylish brown stallion which became one of the most familiar figures on Edmonton streets and avenues. If more were needed to warrant a place of honor on the pages of Canadian history, Prince was the horse chosen to lead the parade on that memorable day when the province of

Alberta was born. Without in any way slighting the many outstanding leaders who participated in the parade, somebody remarked that Prince "practically stole the show."

But long before the parade of September 1, 1905, Prince would have been accepted as the most popular horse personality in Edmonton. His specialty was in delivering parcels of meat from Joe Humble's butcher shop, a role he seemed to enjoy. Like his owner, Prince was born in Ontario, but in coming to Alberta, horse and man followed totally different routes. Joe Humble, born in 1882, accompanied parents from Ailsa Craig, Ontario, to Michigan and then to homestead southwest of Leduc. At the tender age of fifteen, Joe wanted to take a homestead for himself but authorities said he was too young. In his determination, he "squatted" on a quarter section of government land and built a cabin. At sixteen he was breaking and preparing some of the land for cultivation. Later, when he could meet age requirements, he made formal entry for the quarter section on which he had established a moral rather than a legal claim. But in 1898, the Humbles moved to live south of Strathcona and the young fellow formed a closer association with the Edmonton community. He turned to draying on the Edmonton streets and recalled hauling stones and gravel for the construction of the first Imperial Bank building at Jasper Avenue and 100th Street.

Early in 1905, Joe Humble bought Bill Howie's butcher shop, two doors east of the Queen's Hotel and in acquiring the store, he acquired, also, a covered democrat used in making deliveries. Every meat merchant of that time was expected to maintain a horse-drawn delivery cart or wagon and employ a "butcher-boy" to drive it. Needing a suitable horse for the service, Joe Humble's search led to the beautiful brown stallion, Prince, which he bought from a former mounted policeman for seventy-five dollars.

With glistening dark coat and white face, the horse looked and acted like an aristocrat. Although his pedigree could not be confirmed, it was evident that he was part Thoroughbred and had enough style and quality to make him distinctive in any frontier town. He weighed about 1,100 pounds and stood 15 hands.

Most of the meat merchant's customers, lacking refrigeration in any form, wanted their beef and pork parcels brought to their doors on a daily basis and Prince made the rounds with all the regularity of a boy delivering daily papers. Going over the ground day after day, the understanding horse got to know the stops as well as the driver knew them, and when the first butcher-boy was replaced, Humble could tell the new hand to "give Prince his head and he'll take you to the homes where parcels must be left."

The old horse knew how to find the smooth stretches on Edmonton's unimproved streets and avenues and to avoid the potholes and protruding stones. He knew his friends, some of whom carried handfuls of oats in their pockets for the moments when they would meet. Children pulled grass for him and he nuzzled them gently as if to say: "Thanks." He did not like barking dogs and was always suspicious of the Joe H. Morris automobile, the first horseless carriage in Edmonton, and gave it plenty of room when the terrible roar of its two-cylinder motor signaled its approach. But the butcher-boy's horse was never known to have run away or created trouble on the town thoroughfares.

It took only that combination of friendliness and style and good sense to win the attention of people in

Edmonton. Nobody was surprised, therefore, that the committee organizing the parade to mark the birth of a province turned to Prince as the horse to take the foremost position, to carry the parade marshal and the flag. Edmonton people approved.

People in and about the town were excited over plans for inauguration day. They had waited long and a bit impatiently for this day. Yielding to demands from Territorial leaders, Prime Minister Sir Wilfrid Laurier, on February 21, 1905, introduced the Autonomy Bill in the House of Commons to provide for two new provinces and, after long debate, the Act was passed, to come into effect on the following first of September. Regina would be the capital of the province of Saskatchewan and Edmonton was named as provisional capital of Alberta, where the final choice would be left to the new legislature. G. H. V. Bulyea was appointed to the post of Lieutenant-Governor in Alberta and A. E. Forget in Saskatchewan.

But if Ottawa dignitaries like Governor General Earl Grey and the Prime Minister were to be present for the inauguration ceremonies at both capitals, the events would have to be on different dates. Accordingly, September 1 was the inaugural day in Alberta, September 4 in Saskatchewan.

The early autumn sun shone brilliantly as Alberta people donned their best clothes for the celebration. Farmers living within driving distance came to town with buggies and wagons, and many Calgary citizens, still hoping their city would become the capital, came north by train. Realizing that it might be many years before they would have another opportunity of seeing a governor general and a prime minister riding in open carriages, they were not going to miss this one.

14

The parade, a feature of the day's program, was assembled near the Alberta Hotel, on Jasper Avenue, heading west. Spectators lined both sides of the route. Some men sat on the plank sidewalks but the women, anxious to avoid exposing either their ankles or boottops, remained standing. The parade was a fine frontier effort — with Indians, Red River carts carrying pioneers, mounted police, Boer War veterans, bands, floats, Edmonton's first automobile, which had made its original appearance one year earlier, and the visiting personalities: Governor General and Lady Grey, Prime Minister Sir Wilfrid Laurier, Hon. William Paterson, author Sir Gilbert Parker and the newly appointed Lieutenant-Governor Bulyea. And leading all was the well-known Prince, with a military saddle, carrying Sergeant Ted Lessy, a Boer War man, who supported a big flag.

When the signal to start the parade was sounded, Prince was immediately transformed into something with more pride and brilliance than Edmonton people had seen before. He crested his masculine neck, carried his tail with a jaunty flourish and flexed his joints to prance gaily. At once, he seemed like something created to lead a parade and spectators cheered.

After moving westward on the avenue, the parade groups made their way down the hill to terminate at a big tent set up on the flat ground of the broad bench above the river. It would be somewhat west of the 101st Street Edmontonians got to know, roughly between the Donald Ross School and Ortona Armoury of later years. There the speech-making and inaugural formalities took place. There the new Lieutenant-Governor took the oath of office and Alberta was proclaimed a Province.

There was more speech-making, followed by games and a Mounted Police Musical Ride on ground where Renfrew Athletic Park was located later. But customers had to have their meat, and Prince, after completing his part in the parade exercise, went back to work. Little wonder that Prince became more and more a favorite on Edmonton streets.

4

May W

Born to be a Winner

Around the beginning of the present century, a little bay Thoroughbred mare known as May W was the darling of the western racing world. She was something of a surprise package; most people did not expect a mare foaled on the fresh soil of the western frontier, where cayuses were the dominant kind, to become an international racing figure. But May W had good bone and muscle, and the fighting spirit to be a champion. After winning extensively on Canadian tracks, she went on to do the same in the best United States races. So good was her racing record and her conformation that even the breeders in England, home of the Thoroughbred, coveted her. Ultimately, she was shipped to the Old Country, there to be used as a brood mare for breed improvement.

James Speers, undisputed authority on Thoroughbreds, said he regarded her as the best of all
Thoroughbreds produced in Canada.

The story of May W should not be separated
from that of her mother, Froila, one of the true
pioneers among Thoroughbreds in the prairie country. The older mare's story was like something written for a Western movie.

Carrying the name of Sangaroo before being renamed Froila, this Montana mare was at Calgary for
races in the autumn of 1889. Or was it 1890? She was
one of four or five horses owned by an American,
Reynolds by name. It appears that racing luck was
not with the owner during that particular week or that
he simply lived too lavishly and overspent, something which is not unknown in racing circles. Anyway, he ended the week with a substantial deficit and
the Calgary sheriff was seizing his horses to satisfy
the debt. The horseman was distraught. He knew he
should not have borrowed money and spent so reck-
lessly but now the thought of losing his precious
horses was almost more than he could bear.

With a strong feeling of affection for his horses,
this Montana man was ready to do almost anything to
save them from the sheriff's sale. Moreover, he believed that he had not been allowed enough time to
meet the debt and would, therefore, be justified in
trying to steal the animals away from the legal authorities, in the hope of getting them back to his home
quarters south of the border.

But how could this be done? Was there any hope
of finding some knowledgeable and able fellow who
would undertake to whisk the horses away during the
hours of darkness when other Calgary citizens were
still asleep? If he could find such a daring horseman
— one who knew the back trails — the Montana man

would do his part to get the drive started, hoping that the horses could be moved quickly into his home state and beyond the reach of the local sheriff. But how could he find a man who could and would undertake such a long and dangerous drive?

A friend whispered that the best man for such a task would be Tom Lynch, of High River. Lynch, the acknowledged King of the Cattle Trails, had driven numerous herds of livestock into the country when ranges were being stocked. He was, beyond doubt, the best man. But would he do it?

Reynolds talked to Lynch and convinced him that he had, in fact, been treated unjustly in not being given enough time to pay the debt. Lynch considered in silence and then said: "Since it is a matter of justice, I'll run your horses back to Montana, but I'd have to get some sort of payment for my time and work."

"I'm sorry, I have no cash," the owner replied, "but I'll tell you what I'm prepared to do: if you can get my little string of horses back to my Montana home, you can have one of them for settlement."

"Can I take my pick?" Lynch asked.

"Oh, I guess so," was the answer. "They are all good but, yes, you can have your choice and bring that one back with you."

"Fair enough," Lynch said as he got up to leave. "I'll be at the corral before daylight tomorrow morning and we'll be well on our way before anybody in these parts is around."

As the first glow of morning light appeared in the eastern sky, Lynch was mounted on his own trusty horse and ready for the drive. "Your ponies will be in Montana day after tomorrow," he called as he rode away. "We'll make our trail through the hills where we won't be noticed."

For the first night, Lynch stopped at the Quorn Ranch on Sheep Creek where big and friendly John Ware was in charge of the ranch horses. The Quorn people had a program for horse improvement and were importing some of the best Thoroughbred stallions available in England. John Ware, who had come out of slavery in the deep South and was now winning respect and friends on the frontier, welcomed the chance to display his favorite, the recently imported stallion, Eagle's Plume. And Lynch, in turn, confided in Ware that he would claim one of the American mares in his string as a reward for taking the little band across the border. "Which one would you choose?" he asked, knowing that Ware was a good judge of horse stock. "I might as well have the best one."

John Ware studied the animals and then pointed to a chestnut mare, saying: "That one would be my mare if I had the choosing. She's got legs like a deer and a face like an angel." Tom Lynch nodded agreement and added, "They call her Sangaroo. I think she's my pick too. She's got the quality."

At the end of the second day of travel, Lynch and his charges camped beside the Oldman River and Piegan Indians came to share his campfire and the evening view of mountains. When night fell on the third day, the horseman knew he was well within the bounds of the state of Montana and would have no difficulty in delivering the horses according to instructions. Not that Lynch was ever worried about making a drive; nobody knew more about handling trail herds than this man who had brought the first livestock for the North West Cattle Company and the first horses and cattle for numerous other ranching enterprises.

The Reynolds horses were delivered in good

order and, with the least possible delay, Lynch claimed the chestnut mare, haltered her, and started back toward home on the Highwood River. Leading Sangaroo, he had lots of time to study the mare's conformation and disposition and the longer he gazed at her, the better he liked her. "I've got a lot of racing for you back home, young lady," he was saying to her. "We'll show those Bow River cayuses what a real race horse can do and we should pick up a few easy dollars doing it."

Tom Lynch loved a horse race, especially when he had a winner in it. He raced his new mare at many places in the Territories and then sold her to Duncan Cameron who got his mail at Butte, Montana, but who spent a good deal of his time at Calgary. And it was at Calgary in 1894 that Sangaroo, renamed Froila, gave birth to a filly foal, soon to be christened May W. The baby was a dark bay and showed re-fined limbs and a sweet disposition. With Froila for her mother and the great Eagle's Plume for father, inherited speed could have been expected but only time would tell how she would perform in racing. Her first test came when she raced as a two-year-old at Anaconda and won quite easily. She liked to run, seemed to enjoy a race as much as Tom Lynch enjoyed one.

But just as Froila's life was marked by strange twists of fortune and misfortune, so her daughter was not to escape without some trying experiences. A little later in her first season of racing, she was stolen from stables at Butte, Montana. The thieves covered their tracks well and for a time it appeared that May W could be forgotten. Then, unexpectedly, the mare was located at Havre, presumably abandoned by horse thieves heading for the Canadian Border. Obviously, the culprits knew a good horse when they saw one or they would not have been so determined to get May W.

Anyway, she was uninjured and when returned to the track, she continued racing in the best Thoroughbred company and continued winning purses and recognition. What a record she established! In the course of 114 races, she won 43 times, was second 28 times and third 18 times.

And then, the finest compliment of all was that Old Country breeders, ever anxious to maintain and improve the high standard of their Thoroughbreds, wanted May W. Lots of Thoroughbred horses had crossed the Atlantic westward but May W was one of the very few to cross in the opposite direction. And, as had been hoped, the spirit of May W was transmitted to progeny and some of her descendants were brought from England to Canada. The well-known racing mare, Virginia Fair, bred by James Speers, of Winnipeg, and foaled in 1950, was a great-great-granddaughter of May W. Tom Lynch would have loved her too.

Froila and her daughter lived dangerously but they earned honored places in Canadian horse history.

5

Custer

The Old Gray War Horse

If horses could talk, an old gray, ultimately called Custer, might have told a most unusual story of having been owned, successively, by the United States Cavalry, Sioux Indians of Sitting Bull's band, Canadian half-breeds in the Wood Mountain district and, finally, the North West Mounted Police.

The horse was foaled in 1867 — Canada's Confederation Year — but, otherwise, not much is known about the animal's origin. Being of refined type, there was a suggestion this fellow was raised in Kentucky where many of the best horses were secured for cavalry purposes. Anyway, this one was assigned to the U.S. 7th Cavalry and trained to walk, trot and canter in military formations. In due course, the young horse was sent away to the Northwest for war service where Indians were resisting the advances of the white man's possessive ways. Like the life of a soldier, that of a soldier's horse wasn't an easy one; there were long marches, cold nights in the open, prolonged spells between meals, and dangerous skirmishes with cruel enemies.

But abruptly, the gray horse's service in the United States Cavalry ended. It was on the fateful afternoon of June 25, 1876; it was the day of disaster for General George Custer and his column of brave men; it was the day of the so-called Custer Massacre at Little Big Horn River in Montana — last of the major Indian victories against the invading white newcomers.

There had been numerous frontier skirmishes in the West. Sometimes the Indians triumphed, sometimes the whites. Sooner or later there'd have to be a showdown and, understandably, the Indians were ready to fight to the death rather than give up their wild freedom. The Sioux — considered most ferocious of the plains tribesmen, were known to be gathering for a stand in the Wolf Mountain country and the United States military leaders planned a movement to trap them and force them back to their reserves.

General John Gibbon was to march from the north; General George Crook would come from the south, and General Custer would approach from north and east, with all meeting at the confluence of the Big Horn and the Little Big Horn rivers. They were to avoid any major campaign against the Indians until after their union.

Custer, however, encountered fresh signs of Indian encampment and was eager to pursue. Ignoring the fact that his men and horses were fatigued, he divided the force into three columns and assigned three different routes in the hope of intercepting the

Sioux. Warnings from scouts that the Indians were massing in huge numbers went without notice. Custer was an old hand in fighting Indians and was ever eager for the smoke of battle. He had no love for Indians, just as the Indians had no love for him.

With just a few more than 200 mounted men on tired horses, Custer encountered Sitting Bull's painted warriors — more than 2,000 of them — ready for battle. Hopelessly outnumbered, Custer's army was quickly encircled. Shouting and shooting, the natives galloped round and round. The slaughter was terrible. Except for one Indian scout who escaped, nobody on Custer's side remained alive. Dead were 212 brave men. Most of the cavalry horses suffered the same fate, but not all. The Indians had no particular reason for killing horses after the soldiers were annihilated and at least one — the gray nine-year-old — was caught by an Indian and claimed as a prize of war. The Sioux were expert horsemen and recognized superior horses when they saw them. The gray's new owner was happy with his prize.

There was feasting and dancing to celebrate the victory but the Indians moved about uneasily, knowing bigger and stronger United States forces would be sent to inflict punishment. And, just as they expected, their scouts brought word of fresh armies advancing upon them.

Sitting Bull was wise enough to know he could not withstand the full might of the United States government. But what could his people do? A few members of the tribe fled northward and then, in desperation, Sitting Bull led the great mass of his people across the International Boundary — "Medicine Line," as the Indians called it — to be beyond the reach of United States authority. At once the fugitive Indians were the uninvited and unwanted

guests of Canada. The new situation was filled with
danger and Canadian settlers were worried. Government men wondered how the added thousands of
Indians would find food, and Canadian Indians were
openly resentful at the intrusion upon their hunting
grounds.

There was nothing good about it. RCMP Assistant Commissioner Irvine and Superintendent
Walsh, when calling on Sitting Bull, saw warriors
carrying United States army carbines and scalps
taken from men of the Custer force. For four years
thereafter, United States and Canadian authorities
tried to persuade the fugitives to return to their side
of the boundary and, finally, about the middle of
1881, they accepted assurances and went back.

In the meantime, horse stealing and horse trading
were popular occupations around Wood Mountain
where Sitting Bull's people had been camping. The
district was already the home of many Métis people
who had moved from Red River after Louis Riel's
unconstitutional government ended in failure. The
half-breed people, in moving west, had two reasons
— to be closer to buffalo herds and farther from the
objectionable white men.

In the course of horse dealings at Wood Mountain, the good gray gelding which had survived the
Custer Massacre, passed from his Sioux owner to a
local half-breed in a trade. The widely experienced
animal proved to be a good buffalo runner as well as a
good mount for the long journeys to visit friends on
the South Saskatchewan River, north of where
Saskatoon stands today.

By chance, the better-than-average gray horse
caught the eye of Superintendent Walsh one day
when the officer was at Wood Mountain. Walsh
stopped to inspect the animal and talk with the rider.

To his surprise, he noticed the U.S. army brand and, having seen U.S. army rifles which he supposed were taken from Custer's fallen soldiers, he concluded at once that here was a horse taken in the same way. Walsh inspected the horse's mouth and observed the age to be twelve years. Hiding his interest as much as possible, he asked if the horse was for sale. Wood Mountain people, who seldom saw real money, were interested in selling anything and a price was named. Walsh bought the horse, then saw the animal stabled with the mounted police stock where the old warrior would be assured of good feed and care.

Then, as recorded by John Peter Turner in *The North-West Mounted Police, 1873-1893*, Walsh wrote to General Terry of the United States army, reporting his purchase of a horse bearing the Cavalry brand and saying: "If your government or any officer of the 7th Cavalry wishes to have him, I will hand him over, but of the many relics I have seen of the battle on the Little Big Horn, none has taken my fancy like this old trooper, and having been for years an admirer of the gallant Custer, and having conversed with the principal chiefs who took part in that memorable battle, to be permitted to keep this old trooper which has come so strangely into my hands, would be a great pleasure."

Back came a reply, advising that the Secretary of War authorized Major Walsh to keep the horse. Walsh was happy and the old gray, with the amazing and varied record of adventure, became the superintendent's personal saddle horse. With the new name of Custer, the horse lived many years and was treated, quite appropriately, like a war hero.

6

White Wings

Pride of the Calgary Fire Brigade

Every child and every adult in early Calgary was on good terms with White Wings, the gray mare which spent most of her long life with the city's fire department. That was long before the big red fire trucks were known. The quickest way to get firemen and ladders and hose reels to the scene of a fire was with well-trained and fast horses. Nobody wanted a fire but the people in every city took pride in the good horses which, like the firemen, stood by at the firehall, ready to answer an alarm and dash away.

Consequently, horse stalls and hay storage space were part of every firehall and the horses living there soon learned exactly what they were supposed to do when a bell sounded and called them to duty. Everything was planned to get the fire wagons away with the least delay. When a building was burning, each second of time was important. It wouldn't do to waste time in harnessing and hitching, and the firefighters of those years found ways of getting away quickly. The harness, instead of being hung on hooks behind the horse stalls, was suspended from the firehall ceiling, right in front of the wagons.

At the moment a bell sounded the alarm, the doors to the horses' stalls swung open, and the horses trotted out to stand in their proper places under the suspended harness. Then, all in an instant, firemen pulled the ropes which let the harness drop on the horses' backs and just as soon as a few buckles were fastened and drivers could climb onto their seats, the understanding animals dashed away at a fast gallop.

There was no such thing as a siren at that time but every wagon had a bell which the driver could ring by pressing his foot against a pedal. The clear peal of the bells coupled with the drumlike sound of galloping feet on hard streets — and the rattle of wagon wheels — made an impression which nobody standing near-by could ever forget.

After arriving at the scene of the fire, the horses would stand patiently, sometimes in the heat of a blazing summer sun, sometimes in the extreme cold of winter. Always, the understanding of those well-trained and faithful horses made everybody love them.

In Calgary, White Wings was the undisputed favorite. As a young animal, raised on the foothills grass of the Quorn Ranch, she had been a dark gray in color. At three years of age she had been broken to saddle and then to harness. A short time later, Fire Chief James Smart, of the Calgary Fire Department, drove by buggy to the ranch, hoping to buy two horses to be trained for fire wagon use.

Up until that time, Calgary was small, with not enough fire calls to justify keeping horses on hand all the time. The earliest arrangement was that the first team of horses to reach the firehall and be hitched to the ladder wagon after a fire alarm sounded — regardless of who owned the animals — would qualify for five dollars. That was a reward worth running for and every time there was an alarm, either day or night, horse owners and their teams joined in a race from many parts of the town.

By the next plan, Calgary had a city-owned team which served several purposes: part time hauling garbage and, when needed, on fire brigade work. However, the community was becoming bigger and so the city fathers authorized "Cappie" Smart to buy two horses to be kept exclusively for the fire wagon.

Cappie was looking for animals which would be able to run like race horses and, at the same time, have high intelligence so they could be trained easily. He chose two dark grays and his selection proved to be good. They were driven the twenty-odd miles to Calgary, and for the rest of their lives, their home was at the firehall at Sixth Avenue and First Street East. They were named Wings and West Wind and soon learned what they were supposed to do.

They were stylish horses with heads held high and nimble feet. And their speed in getting men and equipment to fires saved the city people from some heavy losses. This was the team which thrilled thousands of visitors attending the big Dominion Exhibition held at Calgary in 1908. Cappie Smart agreed to place these smart animals on display in front of the grandstand. The horses were released in the field inside the racetrack and a fire wagon with harness hung in front of it was placed on the track. With a crowd of several thousand people sitting in the grandstand, a familiar fire alarm bell pealed its message. The two intelligent horses stopped grazing, raised their heads long enough to locate the red wagon they had pulled so often, then dashed to it. Even a cheering crowd was not enough to make these faithful horses take their minds away from duty. They galloped to the red wagon and stood long enough for the harness to be dropped and fastened, then bounded away around the race track looking for the fire. No doubt the horses were annoyed to find it was just another false alarm.

West Wind died and Cappie Smart decided to use Wings to draw a one-horse chemical cart. By this time, the aging mare, becoming lighter in color, was given the name of White Wings. Her new cart was not heavy and with an ever-eager spirit, she could outrun the horses with the big wagons and be first at the fire.

On one occasion, White Wings' driver fell off the cart as it was being drawn away from the firehall. But the old mare knew there should be no delays when a building was burning and she did not stop to collect the fallen fireman; she simply dashed on and didn't slacken her pace until she was at the scene of the fire, along with the other horses from her hall.

When work at a fire was completed and horses and men and equipment were ready to return to the firehall, White Wings usually led the way. She knew the streets and avenues about as well as the firemen and was recognized as an expert in finding the shortest route back to the firehall and her stall.

Somebody said that Cappie Smart and White Wings were the best-known names in the entire city's fire service. And no individual — man or horse — in the brigade had more friends than the old gray mare. Men, women and children going to the scene of a fire

31

often paused along the way to pull some tender bits of grass for their favorite. Regularly at Christmas time, the well-known mare received gifts through the mail, sometimes sugar, sometimes a new brush or curry comb, and at least once a new blanket.

Like a good fireman, White Wings never failed to answer the call of duty with all the energy she possessed.

7

Brownie

James Walker's Faithful Mare

Brownie was a police mare, generally carrying the saddle of Superintendent James Walker, one of the "original" members of the North West Mounted Police. During her first years in the service, she had only an identifying number but in time she won respect, affection, and a name.

James Walker was a horseman in the finest sense. He liked good horses and he knew how to handle the other kind. When the new Mounted Police Force for service in the Far West was being recruited in 1873, he was given the responsibility of selecting and caring for the horses to be taken along. It was perfectly obvious that the success of the new law enforcement officers would depend very largely upon horses and police skill in using them.

Accompanying the 217 officers and men leaving Toronto on June 7, 1874, were 244 horses and an additional 34 were added at Detroit. Men and horses would travel by train to Chicago, St. Paul and Fargo in the United States, and from the latter point in North Dakota, they would go by trail to Fort Dufferin in southern Manitoba. At Fort Dufferin there would be a brief pause for preparations before starting on the great overland trek westward to build a police outpost at some point near the foothills.

Four horses died or played out before reaching Dufferin, leaving 274 eastern horses for the long and difficult journey across unsettled and unsurveyed prairie country. But before getting away from Dufferin, the great pioneer Mounted Police Force came close to losing the entire band. Only the presence of mind and endurance of James Walker saved his friends from the embarrassment of being mounted policemen with nothing to mount.

The near tragedy came during the first night at Dufferin. A violent thunderstorm with heavy hail broke over the camp. Thunder sounded like cannon fire and flashes of lightning broke the darkness. Wind of gale proportions overturned wagons and flattened some of the tents in which men were sleeping. Nothing more was needed to fill the eastern horses with frantic fear and they dashed blindly against the side of their corral, knocking it to the ground. The night guard on duty was helpless and was glad to get out of the path of the desperate animals dashing into the darkness. As they stampeded away from the corral, some ran over tents and tent ropes, and tent occupants were injured.

Superintendent Walker was not on duty but, sensing trouble, he bounded from his camp bed, and as a flash of lightning made everything in the area as bright as day he saw what was happening. As one of the stampeding horses stumbled over tent ropes, he seized its mane and mounted and was, at once, riding through the darkness and storm at a mad gallop. With the storm centered in the north, the stampede was southward.

Over the horse he was riding without either saddle or bridle, Walker had no control but he was determined to stay with the frantic animals until the storm ended. Only in that way would he know where the horses were and have any reasonable chance of gathering them for return to the camp. Fortunately, the horses remained together fairly well.

On and on they ran with every fresh peal of thunder bringing renewed determination to get away from it. An hour passed and Walker figured he was about twenty miles from Fort Dufferin and somewhere in United States territory. Two hours passed and the fatigued horses were still running. And then the storm ended and morning came with a clear sky. Walker was tired, just like the horses, and he did not know exactly where he was. Now, however, he had an opportunity of gathering the horses and herding them back to the camp. It did not escape his notice that the animal he had been riding, a brown mare, had shown remarkable endurance and, even in the dead of night, given him a good ride. He patted her sweating neck admiringly and felt an attachment for her.

Using parts of his suspenders he converted the halter the mare was wearing to a makeshift bridle so that he might control her better. He was then ready to start rounding up the straggling animals and turning them in what he supposed was the direction of Fort Dufferin.

There was now no hurry. The horses were allowed to graze as they traveled slowly in a northeasterly direction. There was an abundance of feed for the horses but no food for Walker. But he pushed on, thankful that he seemed to have most of the horses and thankful for the good fortune of having caught a tireless horse when the storm broke during the night. His fondness for the little brown mare which had carried him over the dark and dangerous course without mishap was mounting. To spare her further fatigue, he caught another horse and then another but he made up his mind that the brown mare with unusual wind and spirit was one he would ride again.

The return drive to Fort Dufferin ended exactly twenty-four hours after it started. Police officers, worried and embarrassed at the prospect of being horseless at this crucial stage in their plan, were delighted to see Walker and his charges. Once back in the camp corral, the horses were counted. Only one was missing.

Mounted Police Commissioner French had compliments for Walker and wished he could reward him suitably. The young superintendent replied that, with the commissioner's approval, he was assigning the game and untiring brown mare to himself. When French nodded, Walker said: "Thanks. Nobody rides her except me from now on."

The great cavalcade of mounted men, wagons, carts, cannons, oxen and machines left Dufferin on July 8, to thread its way across 800 miles of unmarked plains. The hardships were many. Horses suffered and some died. But after ninety-seven days on the trail, men and horses camped beside the Oldman River where a new post, Fort Macleod, would be built.

Superintendent Walker was instructed to start a detachment at Battleford, and then, in 1880, he was transferred to Fort Walsh in the Cypress Hills. The brown mare went along, of course. She was still Walker's favorite. In making the trip to Fort Walsh, the route was by Fort Edmonton and Fort Macleod, roughly 700 miles by trail. But, soon after arrival at Fort Walsh, James Walker was called to Ottawa and the absence was one of several weeks. The mare, by this time known as Brownie, was unhappy; she missed her master and she did not like the strange surroundings. She was homesick and ready to do something about it. When James Walker returned from the East, he was informed that his mare had disappeared. Nobody could understand how it happened. No doubt there were people who would have liked to steal her but there was no evidence of theft. And a search of the near-by hill country failed to produce a trace.

Walker instructed that the search be continued; but weeks passed and there was no clue. Then, to everybody's surprise, a report came from Battleford, where James Walker had been in charge for four years, that his brown mare had wandered in from the prairie, and when the gate was opened, she forthwith went to the stable and entered the stall she had occupied for those years.

What course the mare had followed in making her way from Fort Walsh to Battleford, nobody would ever know. Nor could anybody recall a time when Walker had traveled directly between Fort Walsh and Battleford. There she was, however, at the end of a journey of several hundred miles at best, having demonstrated the wonder of animal instinct. And, as far as Brownie was concerned, she was Back Home and glad to be there.

Having returned from Ottawa with a decision to leave the North West Mounted Police after six years of service in order to manage the new Cochrane

Ranch, Walker knew he could not take Brownie with him and ordered that she should remain at Battleford, which seemed to be her choice.

8

Midnight

Born to Buck

Jim McNab's black gelding, Midnight, when seen running with other range horses on a Porcupine Hills range in southwestern Alberta, appeared so docile and friendly that visitors wanted to talk to him and rub his soft nose. But such an expression of gentleness could be misleading because here was one of those horses with dual personality, capable of good behavior and capable, when occasion demanded, of being a proper rebel. When Midnight felt the annoyance of a bucking strap on his flank or considered the time opportune to test a cowboy's riding tenacity, he could display a frenzy of high kicking and bucking with all the jolting force that might be expected from a demon monster.

In farming communities, a bucking horse was

unloved and unwanted. Before an unruly horse broke a lot of harness and wrecked farm machinery, the owner sought to sell or trade the troublemaker but nobody would knowingly acquire such a brute. When rodeos became popular, bucking horses were needed and the harder they could buck, the more they were worth for the contests. Just as a cowboy could win championships for riding, a good bucking horse could accumulate points and win championships for his performance.

Pioneers in rodeo talked admiringly about horses like Fox, Grave Digger, Cyclone, Bassano, Dynamite, Tumble Weed, and Alberta Kid. But most of all, they talked about Midnight. It was the view of Pete Knight, of Crossfield — four times a world champion bronco rider and on his way to a fifth championship when killed by a bad horse in California — that Midnight was the greatest bucking horse he had ever saddled.

Midnight's breeder, James Wilton McNab, was born on the Horseshoe Dot Ranch beside the Belly River in southern Alberta and was a friend of Tom Three Persons, the Blood Indian who won world fame by gaining the riding championship at Calgary's first Stampede, in 1912. With an inherited love for ranching, Jim McNab was never far from it. As a young man, he took a partner, A. W. Brusselle, and began operating back in the Porcupine Hills where grass was nutritious and winter chinook winds broke the monotony of cold spells. There in the spring of 1916, the coal-black foal was born to one of McNab's ill-tempered Thoroughbred mares. By this time, Jim McNab was in the Canadian army and on his way to World War I battlefields. Consequently, he did not see this particular colt until his return to the ranch at war's end. Then, looking over the young horses, he spotted the black three-year-old and said: "That fellow should make a good stock horse. I may break him for my own use."

At this stage, there was nothing unusual about the colt except for a little more than average spirit. He displayed the customary objection to being saddled for the first time and broken. His talent for explosive bucking was not at first apparent, although he would, now and then, start a day under saddle with a spell of roughouse contortions to which cowboys did not object strenuously. But it was clear that when he bucked, he did it furiously, "as if to kick a hole in the sky." When he settled down, he was at once a good saddle horse.

When Fort Macleod celebrated the fiftieth anniversary of the founding of the place by North West Mounted Police, Jim McNab supplied rodeo stock, and Midnight, then eight years old, had his first big audience. Cowboy contestants said he was terrific. From there the black horse was taken to Calgary for the 1924 Stampede where he bucked with such devastating force that he unseated every cowboy contestant who drew him.

With a growing demand for dynamic rodeo horse stock, Peter Welsh, of Calgary, was buying up the best animals available. He bought Midnight for $500, an exceedingly high price for a horse at that time. He bought Tumble Weed, the horse which had been runner-up to Midnight at the Calgary show, then Bassano, and another famous performer considered so close to Jim McNab's black gelding in bucking ability that he rated the name: Five Minutes To Midnight.

It was a notable aggregation of bucking horses and United States interests wanted any or all. In 1927, Midnight and his rodeo companion, Five

Minutes to Midnight, were sold to the American rodeo contractors, Vern Elliott and Eddie McCarty, of Wyoming and Colorado.

For the next few years, Midnight was the sensation of the United States rodeo circuits, consistently throwing the best riders in the business, Pete Knight, Earl Thode and Paddy Ryan among them. By 1933, the great Midnight was beginning to show his seventeen years. His heart was as stout as ever but the old legs were not quite so powerful as in other years. After a few contestants succeeded in riding him, owners resolved upon retirement for the aging campaigner. The last public appearance was to be at Cheyenne. There, Turk Greenough won the riding championship and as part of the ceremony, it was planned that Greenough would take the old horse in a special riding event and make it the retirement performance. Midnight, the spectators said, seemed to sense the significance of it all and was not going to retire mildly. It was one of the Canadian horse's finest performances and he convincingly unloaded the champion cowboy.

Retired to the McCarty and Elliott grasslands, the old horse enjoyed comfort and fine care until his death from natural causes at the age of twenty years. After his passing, Midnight's burial place rated a headstone with epitaph:

Under this sod lies a great bucking hoss;
There never was a cowboy he could not toss:
His name was Midnight, his coat black as coal:
If there is a hoss Heaven, please God take his soul.

Although the black bucker from Alberta's Porcupine Hills has been dead for many years, he lives in the memory of rodeo cowboys as the Champion of Them All.

9

Jack

The School Horse

Jack was a gray gelding, not very big, not very fast, not very handsome. He was never in a race or a showring and if he had been offered for sale, he would have commanded no more than the most modest price. Jack possessed qualities which were useful rather than glamorous. He was friendly, faithful and reliable, and with these attributes, he became a specialist and spent the last twelve or fifteen years of his long life transporting children to and from a country school, north of Brandon. One teacher reported that for more than a year, old Jack had perfect school attendance.

The story of his early life became lost and if he knew anything about his pedigree, he treated it as a secret and kept it to himself. With an indistinct brand on his left thigh, it could be presumed that Jack was

43

foaled and raised on a western ranch and was part of a wild and spirited band.

When he appeared in a sales stable in Brandon about 1898, he was a three-year-old bronco, resenting the sudden loss of freedom which came with his removal from the home range. Like other ranch-raised horses, he hated restraint and would fight if humans tried to force anything as strange and objectionable as harness on him. He could strike viciously with front feet and kick hard enough to scare attendants with his hind feet.

Homesteaders had to have power for the heavy toil of field work and they preferred horses to the slow and uninspiring oxen. Farm-raised horses with friendly dispositions were favored but there were not enough of them and they cost more than the lowly broncos. The homesteader who had the courage to take broncos could save on the investment. Also in the bronco's favor was hardiness. Raised under almost natural conditions, the bronco knew how to take care of itself and could live outside in winter better than the heavier and more docile draft horse of Clydesdale or Percheron or Belgian breeding.

Anyway, Jim Grant, who was just getting started on his new farm north of Brandon, needed a horse and was attracted by this three-year-old with the nice dark-gray coat. He knew the young horse had the fighting spirit of a bronco, but thinking that he could master and domesticate the animal, he paid the price of fifty dollars and took him home.

Breaking the new horse was not easy. The bronco tried to run away and tried to kick his way out of harness but the breaking technique consisted of hitching the green horse with one already broken and well trained and the colt discovered that he could not have his way. Gradually, he accepted the hateful bit placed in his mouth, the annoying blinkers fixed on the bridle, the harsh collar fitted to his shoulders and the various straps and bands and traces making up the rest of the harness. Gradually, he became accustomed to working in the fields, doing his share in pulling plows, harrows and seed drills in the spring and binders and grain wagons in the autumn. It was not much fun but fighting the harness and implements only made the work more difficult. Jack was wise enough to sense and accept the inevitable and settle into farm work routine.

For the next few years, Jack was just another farm horse. In time, however, because he was smaller and lighter in the limbs than the other farm horses, he was the one chosen to haul the family buggy to town on Saturdays and to church on Sundays. Jogging on the country roads was not any easier than working in the farm fields but it was a change and the little horse did not mind it. Then, when the farmer obtained more horses, Jack was relieved completely of field work. He became the road horse, hauling buggy in summer and cutter in winter.

More years passed and children on the Grant farm were coming to school age. It was two miles to the local school, rather far for small children to walk morning and night, and it became common practice for one of the adults on the farm to hitch Jack to the buggy or cutter and drive the little ones. Twice a day Jack jogged his way to the country school and back to the farm. He got to know the route and the routine thoroughly and even seemed to enjoy his job.

As the horse grew older, his color changed from dark gray to light gray and his ways became more gentle and lovable. Regardless of who was driving, young person or old, Jack conducted himself exactly the same. It was perfectly safe for the children to hitch and drive to the school without aid from an adult. The horse refused to let the youthful drivers get into trouble. With their immature judgment, the youngsters might very easily have driven the buggy or cutter to collide with a gatepost or turned too sharply and upset the conveyance, but the aging Jack made sure it did not happen.

And then Jack's experience and skill led to a still further responsibility being placed upon him. It was like getting a promotion without an increase in salary. Quite often the farm buggy and buggy horse were needed for other tasks during school hours, making it necessary for horse and vehicle to be returned to home quarters after the children were delivered at school in the mornings. Normally, this would necessitate one of the adults driving the children to school, bringing horse and buggy back for other duties, and then going again for the children in the afternoon. But Jack's owner, with supreme confidence in the knowing old horse being able to handle the situation unattended, instructed that the children drive to school as usual and, then, instead of placing Jack in the school stable, they were to get out of the buggy, tie the reins around the dashboard so they would not fall to the ground, turn horse and buggy around in the direction of home and give Jack the signal to be going. It sounded simple and, sure enough, it worked.

Jack brought the buggy home, alone, and that was not all; half an hour before school would be dismissed for the day, Jack was again hitched to the buggy and, with reins securely looped around the dashboard, he was started toward school, unattended. Knowing exactly what was expected of him, Jack set out at his customary pace, a slow trot, and made his way through the open gates, around corners at road intersections, and back to the school, there to wait patiently until all his little passengers were loaded and ready for the trip back home. It worked so well that, thereafter, neighbors did not even express surprise when they happened to pass horse and buggy, without driver, on the road.

It did not seem to matter if a driver was present or not; Jack was guided by judgment or instinct more than by the tug on a rein. Jack knew what to do and would do it anyway, whether tiny hands were on the reins or not. Young drivers could be distracted but Jack was never distracted. His mind was ever on his work. When confronted with another vehicle coming toward him, he would turn out sufficiently — always to the right — to ensure safe passing.

If at any time a child fell out of the buggy, Jack would stop and remain motionless until the small passenger was back in place. If careless little hands drew too hard on one rein, indicating a dangerous trip into the roadside ditch, Jack would recognize it as an error and refuse to be guided by it.

Children started to public school and finished their formal education with Jack. Others came to school age and did the same. Sometimes there was only one child to be transported; sometimes there were more pupils than the buggy could accommodate and the overflow took places on Jack's back. It did not matter where the youngsters chose to ride, Jack felt responsibility for their safety. He could not prevent a child from falling out of the buggy or off his back but he could ensure against the chance of that child being run over or stepped on. Jack's safety record over a period of a decade and a half was just about perfect.

The old horse, performing his duties with obvious understanding, became as much of a local institution as the one-room country school. It was a sterling performance for a horse which had started out as a protesting bronco.

When the history of education in rural communities is written, there should be proper recognition of the noble part played by old gray Jack and the many other school horses and school ponies which rendered essential services.

10

Sir Barton

Toast of the Racing Circuit

When the Canadian-owned Thoroughbred stallion, Sir Barton, and the United States-owned Thoroughbred stallion, Man o' War, came together for a matched race at Kenilworth Park, beside Windsor, Ontario, on October 12, 1920, it had all marks of a Battle of the Giants. Men on farms and men on city streets speculated alike about the outcome. Cleveland Americans were winning over Brooklyn Dodgers for the pennant in the World Series at the time and promoters were negotiating to match Jack Dempsey and Georges Carpentier in a world championship boxing event. But nothing in the sporting world was claiming more attention than "The Race." Writers called it "The Turf Contest of the Century."

Apart from the international glory attached to victory, there would be a big tangible reward. The prize consisting of $75,000 and a gold cup valued at $5,000 — winner take all — was the richest in North American turf history to that time. Altogether, it promised to be one of the most exciting contests since David met Goliath in the Valley of Elah.

Both stallions had formidable racing records and both were in the pink of track condition when they came to Kenilworth. Sir Barton, owned by Commander J. K. L. Ross, O.B.E., of Montreal, was the Three-Year-Old of the Year in 1919, and Man o' War, owned by Samuel D. Riddle, of Philadelphia, was the Three-Year-Old of the Year in 1920. The matching seemed perfect. Sir Barton was the first to collect the "Triple Crown" in one year, having won the Kentucky Derby, the Preakness, and the Belmont in his big year. And Man o' War's winnings included Preakness, Withers, Belmont, Stuyvesant, and Jockey Club stakes. His only defeat was by Upset, a horse he beat easily on other occasions.

The two noted horses had never met on a track. North American race fans demanded a showdown contest and neither Samuel Riddle nor Commander Ross was a man to refuse a challenge.

The great Man o' War was bred by August Belmont, who was chairman of the Jockey Club. Receiving a wartime commission in 1918, Belmont made himself ready for service by preparing to sell his young Thoroughbreds at public auction. Man o' War was one of those offered but not one of the more popular yearlings. Most buyers had nothing more than a passing glance for the awkward colt and Samuel Riddle bought him for $5,000. It was one of the lower prices of the sale, but after Man o' War had won twenty out of twenty-one races in which he was entered and accounted for purses totaling about a quarter of a million dollars, the purchase price must have been seen as one of the best bargains in horse history.

Commander Ross, on the other hand, was a Canadian — a distinguished Canadian. He was born at Lindsay, Ontario, and after graduating from McGill, he made his home in Montreal where his first job was a lowly one in the car shops of the Montreal street railway. During World War I, he commanded a destroyer doing duty along the Atlantic coast for the Canadian navy and was then attached to a North Atlantic Squadron of the Imperial navy. In postwar years, he became a leader in Canadian industry and in just about everything else to which he gave his attention. For many years he held the record for the biggest Atlantic tuna fish landed with rod and line; his fish weighed 680 pounds. When he became interested in Thoroughbred horses, he brought to them the same brand of enthusiasm which had marked his involvement in mining, railroading, and fishing.

Making huge investments in horses, Ross acquired some outstanding individuals and for two years, 1918 and 1919, he dominated the North American tracks. Cudgel, which led all track rivals in 1918 with prize money totaling $99,000, and Sir Barton and Billy Kelly, which finished first and second respectively in the Kentucky Derby of 1919, were his most famous runners. Winnings by Ross horses in the single year, 1919, came to $209,303, with Sir Barton accounting for the biggest portion.

The chestnut Sir Barton was an American-bred and, like Man o' War, he was a little slow in taking on the appearance of a champion. As a two-year-old, he was not impressive, but as a three-year-old, he was a sensation, just as Man o' War was a sensation a year later.

To settle a million speculative arguments, the two outstanding horses had to meet and race, and the time and place were fixed.

The day of the race arrived. The sun shone brightly on Kenilworth and Canadians could scarcely hide their pride in seeing an international race bringing together two of the greatest horses in the world being staged on Canadian soil. Thirty thousand people crowded into the park to cheer their favorites and some were turned away. In the betting, Man o' War was the favorite.

The race to which everybody was looking forward was scheduled for 3:30 p.m. Man o' War was to be ridden by Clarence Kummer and Sir Barton by Frank Keogh. Sir Barton drew the rail position and actually got away to the better start and led for a short distance. But Man o' War forged ahead and held the lead. Keogh used his whip but Sir Barton could not overtake the rangy Man o' War with the tremendously long running stride. The American horse increased his lead and finally came to the wire about seven lengths ahead of Sir Barton.

There was no doubt about the winner. Man o' War emerged as the Champion of Champions, but nobody thought any less of the Canadian horse. It just was not Sir Barton's day to win. Man o' War set a Kenilworth track record of two minutes and three seconds for the mile and one-quarter but both horses, in previous performances, had made better times for that distance.

A million dollars went through the pari-mutuels that day, more than one quarter of it on the Man o' War-Sir Barton race. But it was an unexciting day for the bettors. Those who bet on Sir Barton, lost their money, and those who bet on Man o' War received $2.10 in return for a $2.00 investment.

Anyway, Man o' War was at once the unchallenged King of the Turf and admiring crowds surged around him. He was allowed to inspect the gold cup donated by the Kenilworth Jockey Club. Both horses posed for pictures and were then led away to their private railway cars to be shipped to home stables and to retirement.

Fancy offers were made for both horses but the animals were not for sale. Riddle was reported to have refused offers as high as $400,000, quite a figure for a horse which had cost him $5,000.

Canadians had hoped to see Sir Barton win but there was no disgrace in being beaten by what many people believed was the greatest Thoroughbred that ever looked through a riding bridle. Commander Ross was praised for his devoted interest in horses and his gameness in entering the most famous international race in North American history.

11

Barra Lad

Greatest Jumper of Them All

Ask any pioneer horseman to name the greatest jumper in Canadian history and, if his memory is good, he will say "Barra Lad," the jumping sensation of the years prior to 1925. The horse made his last jump at New Westminster, on September 12 of that year, a convincing world record for owner, Peter Welsh, of Calgary.

It was during the Golden Age for horses. Every farmer was an expert horseman and every farm boy received a thorough grooming in horsemanship. Hamestraps, bellybands and swamp fever were part of the everyday vocabulary. And western horsemen believed they possessed the breeding resources to produce the best of any kind. The new West had draft horses with world championships, running and trotting horses whose names were as familiar as those of

John L. Sullivan and Ernest Cashel, refined hacks, graceful roadsters, versatile stock horses, and high jumpers as good as could be found anywhere. Among the jumpers, there were Smokey and Rolla G. Kripp and Cerebos and others, great performers, but Barra Lad was still the champion of champions. He was also a strange equine personality, temperamental and explosive in jumping performances.

The Lad was bred at Colony farm, Essondale, British Columbia, a place which became internationally famous for its Holstein cattle. The horse's father was a Hackney, his mother a mare of Standardbred type. The foal was an orphan from birth, but the little fellow was bottle fed and, with help from nurses at the hospital, was soon thoroughly spoiled. That was in 1918.

Before any thought was given to the colt's future, workmen at the farm noticed the bay orphan's readiness to jump logs or barrels rather than walk around them. And before long, no gate was high enough to stop him.

At Calgary, Peter Welsh, who came from Stirling, Scotland, was dealing in horses of all kinds. Reports about this two-year-old colt with unusual jumping propensities reached him and he sent an offer to purchase, $150, sight unseen. The offer was accepted and the young horse was shipped to Calgary, express collect. There, the colt's education was intensified, with Peter Welsh's sons, Louis and Josie, as the teachers. The Lad began to demonstrate his special qualities. Taken to eastern Canada as a three-year-old, he won against experienced horses and the Welsh men began to realize they had a champion.

At the Spring Show in Brandon, 1922, the Calgary entry brought spectators to their feet when fourteen-year-old Louis Welsh took Barra Lad over the bars at six feet, ten inches, to establish a Manitoba record. That was on a Monday night. On Thursday night, Barra Lad shattered his previous record by jumping seven feet, one inch.

The horse's peculiar dispostion could not go unnoticed. In the stall, he was friendly and gentle; "biting or kicking was the last thing he thought about." When being exercised, he would loaf along at three miles an hour without any restraint. But in the arena, the otherwise gentle horse became "a ball of fire." Said Josie Welsh, "Just show him a jump and he'd go mad. There was no holding him."

When Louis Welsh, who normally rode him, was injured and unable to ride at Brandon, it fell to Josie to take him over the jumps. Josie was worried, fearful he might not be able to handle this equine rocket. He asked Louis what he should do and the brother replied: "When you turn him to a jump, just grab a big handful of mane and shut your eyes and let him do the rest." Josie took the advice and said later: "I didn't know I was over the seven-foot bars until I heard the crowd roaring."

During the next three years, Barra Lad, weighing 1,100 pounds and standing 15¾ hands, was a conquering hero at Canadian and United States shows. At a big exhibition near Seattle, he astonished horsemen in that part by clearing the seven-foot jump in each of the seven days of the show. And, then, on April 1, 1925, Calgary people saw the Lad jump seven feet, one inch. It was the last appearance in the horse's home city. The climax to his great career came soon after at New Westminster, where 6,000 people were present at the horse show arena and saw far more than any could have anticipated.

After a jump of six feet which the Calgary horse

took with scornful ease, the bars were raised to seven feet, then to eight feet, one and one-half inches. The measurements were made with special care by men who realized the importance. Some people thought it quite ridiculous to set the jump so high because no horse had ever cleared its equal.

Entering the arena, Barra Lad appeared utterly untamed, as usual. Angrily, he champed on his bit and tossed his head from side to side. He had but one thing in mind, to locate the obstacle and leap over it. With Louis Welsh, then seventeen years old, securely in the saddle and understanding the ill-tempered horse better than any other person, Barra Lad cut short the customary circle at the end of the arena and broke into a mad run toward the bars. With ears back, nostrils distended and muscles collected, the dynamic brute leaped almost catlike into the air. Forefeet went over; momentarily it seemed that he could never get his hind ones over; but, with perfect precision, he pulled the hind feet against his belly and was over without as much as a touch, eight feet, one and one-half inches — a world jumping record. The best previous mark was eight feet and three-sixteenths of an inch, made by a horse in Chicago two years earlier. Six thousand people stood and cheered in astonishment. Everybody knew that horse history was being written. But there was a sad sequel: as the horse came down from the jump, he went on his knees, plowing a tanbark furrow with his distinctive white muzzle. Louis Welsh remained in the saddle and Barra Lad was at once back on all four feet.

There was no reason to think of serious trouble. An enthusiastic crowd surged into the ring to be close to this Champion of Champions. But Barra Lad, even though severely shaken, was inviting neither sympathy nor affection. To him, the jumping ring was no place for nonsense. He wanted no part of spectator adulation.

Taken back to his stall, Barra Lad was given a rubdown and the customary evening ration of rolled oats and bran. Normally, he was a good feeder but on this night he refused his grain. Something was wrong. Something was indeed wrong and in a matter of a few hours, the great horse — greatest jumper of his time — was dead. The cause: internal hemorrhage induced by the shock of that terrific jump. It was a sad moment for members of the Welsh family as it was for all who admired the Barra Lad brand of spirit and fiber.

Appropriately, the body was accorded burial right on the New Westminster Exhibition Grounds, just outside the arena where the great jumper made world history and made many Canadian horsemen very proud.

12

Sandy

Pride of the Princess Pat's

If horses could have qualified for war medals, a gelding remembered by veterans of the Princess Patricia's Canadian Light Infantry would have had an imposing row of them.

Military people in the days of cavalry admired great and courageous horses as they admired great and courageous soldiers but never got around to granting them anything in the way of lasting memorials. But Sandy was one horse which was not to be forgotten. A visitor to the officers' mess of the P.P.C.L.I. in Edmonton would see on a mantle a fancy snuffbox made from the hoof of one of Sandy's feet, a chair covered with leather from Sandy's hide, a picture on the wall showing the old horse during his retirement in Somerset, England, a framed scroll paying glowing tributes to him and, in another building not far away, Sandy's tail and military saddle, kept for purely sentimental reasons.

Sandy was a Canadian horse, a half-bred Thoroughbred with sorrel coat, flaxen mane and tail, one white foot, a white blaze on the face, high withers, flat bone and the general cut for a good hunter. He had been trained for polo and grew to like the game. On the playing field, he was agile and fast; he could "turn on a dime" and brake to a sliding stop.

Sandy was, indeed, one of Gavin Ogilvie's finest polo horses but when the First Great War broke in 1914, such things as polo lost their importance and the horse was presented to the new P.P.C.L.I., to become the personal charger of Major Andrew Hamilton Gault who had just founded the regiment and contributed $100,000 to help in equipping it. Lieutenant-Colonel Francis D. Farquhar was selected to command the new body and it was his suggestion that the regiment be called Princess Patricia's Canadian Light Infantry, honoring the oldest daughter of the Duke and Duchess of Connaught, the Duke being at that time the Governor General of Canada. After only a short stay in Canada, the Princess had endeared herself to the Canadian people and members of the new regiment were proud when she consented to the use of her name.

As second in command, Major Gault went overseas late in 1914 and Sandy went too. Sandy seemed to have exactly the right temperament for a war horse. He was eager and fearless and, as stated on the framed scroll hanging on the P.P.C.L.I. mess wall at Edmonton, he became "a great favorite throughout the Brigades in which he served and was well known at Divisional Corps Headquarters. He was entirely unmoved or almost unmoved under fire which he encountered on various occasions when on reliefs or reconnaissance rides. On at least one occasion he should have been wounded when he came under a bracket of shrapnel fire from the enemy's guns while passing down the Ypres road to the ruined city one fine afternoon after the Regiment's return to the Salient in 1916.''

And like any other good soldier, Sandy liked to have some fun when the work was done and the time was opportune. ''One of his favorite pastimes was to pull off a button or two from the tunic of the orderly who held him, little knowing of his humorous tricks and he was not at all averse to gently nipping the behind of any soldier who was not on the lookout for his blandishments. He was aware that Infantry Officers were not always good horsemen and would never allow a strange rider to force him beyond a trot on the hard paved roads of Flanders but, on getting back to the grass, might wangle in a few bucks which sometimes put the rider out of the 'dish.' ''

Major Gault was wounded for the fifth time at the Battle of Sanctuary Wood on June 2, 1916, and lost a leg. Despite the handicap, he returned to duty as a staff officer and, ultimately, rose to the rank of brigadier. As for Sandy, he was returned to England at the close of hostilities, there to enjoy many years of peaceful but useful service as a hunter. Often he was ridden to hounds and he liked it. When carrying an adult, he could be difficult to handle. Not so when a child was in the saddle; then, Sandy was quiet and gentle and he was the means of teaching many young people the art of riding a hunter horse. The English children loved Sandy.

When the horse was sent overseas at the beginning of World War I, he was said to be twelve years old. That was probably correct. He was a hardy

Canadian specimen and had many years ahead of him. His death at Hatch Court in Somerset, England, in 1935, was that of a veteran of thirty-three years and some P.P.C.L.I. tears were shed for Old Sandy.

No doubt, it was of just such a cavalry horse that Saskatchewan's Captain Stanley Harrison wrote after his faithful animal was killed during the First Great War. The loss of his horse was the loss of a companion, near and dear, and the lines written at Passchendale in November, 1917, would leave no doubt about the attachment and admiration:

"Never shall I forget the first time I saw him there in the hills of home. Head uplifted, his brilliant eyes regarded me with a kindly dignity. Ah, but he was superb! About him was a great shining, like a naked sword tempered in beauty and strength. Beneath his coat of rippling silk one sensed the soul of rhythm, and courage like white fire . . .

"Nor that last hour shall I forget. Even as I caught his low whinney I knew the wings of Pegasus had touched his shoulders. There amid the rumble of guns, Death had beckoned. But there, too, was something greater than death, shining down through the long long trailing centuries of Time . . .

"Beyond the cannon-mist I thought I saw him again, imperishable as all true beauty, one with the wind and sun, one with the glory of life — aye, and the glory of death.

"Remember him.
Somewhere in God's Own Space
There must be some sweet-pastured Place
Where creeks sing on and tall trees grow,
Some Paradise where horses go,
For by the love which guides my pen
I know great horses live again."

13

Old Bill

Faithful and True

Old Bill was no beauty. In fact, he was so ugly that other horses on the MacEwan farm shunned his company. Advanced age showed clearly, but that was not all. His head was too big for his body; his feet were too big for his limbs; his ears pointed in different directions and his legs were decorated with splints and spavins. On top of all that, he suffered from chronic indigestion. But no horse on the western frontier served more faithfully and none deserved a monument more than Old Bill.

The unending toil on pioneer farms was hard on horses, as protruding ribs, raw harness sores and dejected equine spirits showed so clearly. But horses were much more serviceable than oxen and every farmer wanted them. Favored, of course, were the big ones with heavy bone and powerful muscles,

Clydesdales, Percherons and Belgians. Such draft horses could move heavy loads on roads or in farm fields with less hardship to themselves than would be experienced by animals of smaller stature. Obviously, a horse of 1,200 pounds sharing harness with one of 1,700 pounds had to work especially hard to keep its end of the doubletree in line.

Old Bill had that added handicap of being a lightweight, presumably of Standardbred strain although his exact breeding was unknown. In other words, he was of roadster type and ill-suited for heavy draft work. The only reason for buying him to work on that frontier farm was his availability at the price of thirty-five dollars, all the cash the MacEwans were able to raise in a particular hour of need.

Having been delivered to a farm where horsepower was needed urgently, the little bay gelding was introduced at once to heavy harness and teamed with three big horses to pull a breaking plow through tough sod and tenacious willow roots. Day after day, six days a week, Bill tugged hard on leather traces, and on Sundays, when the heavy horses enjoyed a day off, poor Old Bill was burdened with an additional assignment, one which he alone could perform with reasonable satisfaction; it fell to him to pull the family buggy to church. As he was the only horse on the premises with buggy experience and the only one of roadster weight, the weekly trip — four miles each way — was one he could not escape, even though it might have been merciful and even Godly for the humans to have remained at home in order to give one of the Creator's four-footed children a chance to rest and enjoy a day on the grass.

Bill was a tired old horse but his needs were not entirely overlooked and as soon as farm fortunes would allow it, a replacement draft horse was purchased and Bill was released from heavy harness, left with no work except that of pulling the buggy in summer months and the cutter in the winter. At once, life was less cruel and a trace of fat returned to his old ribs.

Like any other aging gentleman, Bill liked his home — liked it so well that his traveling time from the near-by town to the home farm was only about half of what he took in going over the same road but in the opposite direction. In returning from church or town, he did not always wait for his passengers. On a certain Sunday, when the church minister preached too long for the patience of either the people in the congregation or the horses waiting to haul buggies and churchmen home, Bill used his long incisor teeth to loosen the knot which tied him in a livery stable stall and promptly struck out for home, leaving buggy and passengers stranded in Melfort. Neighbors saw the familiar horse, harnessed but without vehicle, making his way over the four-mile road to the MacEwan farm, maintaining the jog he was known to favor on the homeward part of all trips.

With Bill's home-loving nature went an uncanny sense of direction. It did not seem to matter where he was driven, a homing pigeon kind of perception would take him home. Even in the darkest night or when blinding snow filled the air, Bill seemed to know where he would find his stall and manger filled with hay.

There was that winter trip by cutter to a community six or eight miles from the home farm, in the course of which Bill's skill was put to a severe test. Much of the land was still undeveloped and when nightfall and a snowstorm came together, the three occupants of the cutter, setting out for home, felt understandable anxiety. Visibility failed completely and the man driving, trying desperately to guide the horse, unconsciously drew the animal off the trail and into an expanse of bluffs and grassland. Once having left the track, it seemed almost impossible to find it again. In an instant, all sense of direction left the cutter's occupants, No stars were visible to help in guiding them. Realizing that they were lost and probably already driving in a senseless circle, they decided in their despair to "give Old Bill his head" and hope for the best.

The night grew colder and snowdrifts became deeper. It was increasingly difficult to be cheerful. To be lost in the open country on such a night would certainly invite serious freezing and perhaps loss of life. The three men in the cutter understood the dangers very well. They took turns in walking behind the cutter, partly to reduce the load, partly to maintain circulation of blood. The horse abandoned his customary road jog — settled into a slow but steady walk. As the snow became deeper, the animal had to work harder. He was covered with snow and it was impossible to see him, even from the seat of the cutter.

An hour passed and then two hours. The cold was more and more intense. It seemed increasingly certain that Old Bill was as hopelessly lost as the men. The situation appeared ever more terrifying. Perhaps the travelers were now farther from home than when they had started. And how long would it be until the old horse dropped from exhaustion or ran into a barbed wire fence, wrecking cutter and injuring himself?

"If we could only find a strawpile," one man remarked, "we could dig in and hope to stay alive until daylight." Nothing, however, was visible, neither bluffs, fences nor strawpiles. But Bill plodded on and, then, when human hands and feet were almost paralyzed from cold, the cutter stopped abruptly. "What now?" somebody asked. "What trouble have we hit?" The driver stumbled forward to the horse's head and to his amazement, found himself within touching distance of a stable door. "We're home," he shouted. "We're at our stable. God bless you, Bill, you brought us through. We'd never have made it if we hadn't left it to you."

The old horse enjoyed an extra ration of oats that night and regularly for weeks after. He did not get the monument he and thousands of other farm horses deserved but he did get the comfortable retirement he had earned so completely. Farm fortune improved and the debt to Bill was at least partly paid, paid with the best care that could be given to an old horse which had worked hard and faithfully.

14

Queenstown

The Gallant Old Friend

Ask almost any pioneer rancher from the Alberta Foothills if he remembers Queenstown, and he will probably answer, "Yes, indeed, everybody out there knew Herbert Eckford's big gray gelding. I tell you that horse saved so many men from drowning, he should have had a gold medal for lifesaving."

Some horses distinguished themselves in the showring, some on the race track, some in rodeo and so on, but Queenstown's special knack was swimming and he loved to do it. Rivers in those years before there were bridges, it should be understood, presented many problems for travelers. When river levels were low, men might ford them or simply wade across, but in seasons when those streams were in flood, a traveler either swam or abandoned hope of crossing. If swimming a fast and flooded river was attempted, the risk was high and many people lost their lives by drowning. Having a horse that was good at swimming was a big advantage, but not all were good swimmers. Just as with people, some horses were proficient swimmers and some were failures.

With stock grazing on both sides of the Highwood River, Queenstown's owner found it necessary to cross the stream countless times. When the water was too deep for fording, the horseman might remain in the saddle and let Queenstown carry him to the other side; a safer way was to start his horse on the proper course and then slide off to seize the animal's tail and be pulled through the water. Even when pieces of ice were floating in the river, the faithful horse never faltered. Queenstown gained a reputation and neighbors, facing the necessity of crossing at high water and unwilling to trust their own horses, would borrow the reliable gray, and breathe their gratitude.

Queenstown, according to the people who knew him, "could swim like a beaver." But that was not his only distinction; he was a great and reliable stock horse which won the admiration of everybody who knew him. At twenty-five years of age — at which time he was completely white — he was still his owner's favorite mount.

Foaled in the state of Washington in 1882, this horse was an immigrant to the Canadian range. He was five years old — still unbroken to saddle or even halter — when driven overland to the Foothills. Having been bred on the American range, his exact pedigree was unknown except that he was believed to carry both Percheron and Thoroughbred bloodlines. No doubt his gray color came from the Percheron in his pedigree and the graceful bearing and quality from the Thoroughbred. He was tall — about 16 hands — and heavy enough to be a useful general-purpose farm horse or a heavyweight hunter.

Queenstown's Canadian home throughout his long life was the High River Horse Ranch, started by Duncan McPherson and Major Haldane Eckford in 1887, immediately after the awful winter of 1886-87 in which fully a quarter of all the cattle on the western range perished. There existed a general impression that horses would withstand bad winters better than cattle and ranchers should change their production patterns accordingly. Consequently, these two young ranchers imported four high-class Thoroughbred stallions from England and then arranged with Tom Lynch, King of the Old Cattle Trails, to bring 600 horses from the state of Washington. It would be a case of driving the wild band overland all the way to the Canadian range. Often the Lynch job was to drive 3,000 cattle from Montana or Idaho to some destination in the new Canadian ranching country and nobody could do it with more skill. On this occasion, 500 of the horses were for breeding purposes on the High River Horse Ranch and 100 were to be retained by Lynch. In the band were two gray horses which the pioneers could never forget, Grey Eagle, which became the most famous race horse of his time, and Queenstown, soon to distinguish himself in other ways.

As Herbert Eckford — son of one of the ranch owners — remembered the imported horses, they were all as wild as the wind. As might be expected, a few were conspicuous by spirit and appearance and quality, and one of these was the gray to be known as Queenstown. The younger Eckford resolved to break this one for his own use. Contrary to what had been expected, the horse was not difficult to break to

70

saddle and the young man knew he had made a good choice.

Between man and horse there grew a lasting companionship. For twenty years, Queenstown was Herbert Eckford's saddle horse for range work, pleasure riding, and hunting coyotes. With endurance, speed when it was needed, sure-footedness and understanding in performing cutting work, the horse was unusually versatile. He seemed to know exactly what his owner wanted him to do, and that was what the horse wanted to do.

Speaking many years after the horse's death, the owner could say: "Queenstown saved my life on more than one occasion and also the lives of other men." The animal's lifesaving service was mainly in the water. There was that early summer day when Herbert Eckford mounted his gray gelding with the idea of riding to a remote part of the range but immediately heard frantic calls for help coming from the direction of the flooded Highwood. Turning to investigate, he saw a team of runaway horses, wet and dragging a doubletree, dash up the bank from the river. Obviously the team had become disengaged from a wagon, but where was the wagon? Looking more carefully, he saw the wagon at a midpoint in the river, with two frightened men sitting on top of the heavy load, busily engaged in shedding boots and clothing to be ready for the awful plunge when the wagon toppled in the boiling stream. From their display of fear, it was rather obvious that neither could swim. Knowing that only he and Queenstown could help the stranded men, Eckford studied the dangerous situation, all the while galloping toward the water.

The circumstances became clear. The wagon had become stuck during the attempted crossing and the horses had gained their release when, in the course of their wild plunging, the pin holding the doubletree had become disengaged. Eckford headed his horse into the river and toward the wagon and Queenstown seemed to understand. When close to the stranded wagon, Eckford called for the men, one at a time, to leap to catch Queenstown's tail. Having pulled the first of the unfortunate fellows to shallow water, horse and rider turned and again fought the swirling water to recover the second victim in exactly the same way. No sooner was the second man brought to safety than the wagon trembled and then capsized in the wild current. Only with a willing horse like Queenstown, Eckford said, could the recovery have been carried out and the two lives saved.

On another day, as Eckford confessed, his horse saved his life. It was early in the spring, before the breakup but not before the ice was weakened by thawing. The rancher crossed the river in the morning without recognizing signs of danger, but when returning after a day of riding, he found water running over the ice, several inches deep. He knew there was risk in crossing but he was anxious to get home and would take the chance.

To attempt crossing was a mistake and about halfway over, a big piece of ice broke loose and horse and rider dropped into the channel. The horse went down to strike the bottom and then bounced to the surface, giving Eckford the chance to leap over the animal's head to land on firm ice. In making his jump to safety, the man carried the reins with him. The horse went down again but Eckford braced himself to help his friend. Again the horse surfaced and as he did, he jumped; with his owner tugging with all his strength on the reins, the animal managed to land on the ice, which proved strong enough to hold him. It was a case of the horse saving the man and the man saving the horse and Eckford gave Queenstown most of the credit.

"Most horses," Eckford said, "would not have tried to come out after the break into the icy water, but not so with Queenstown, whose courage and stamina saved us both."

The rancher had ridden many horses but never another like his old gray. When the animal was twenty-five years old and still his favorite mount, Mr. Eckford could say that Queenstown had never been sick, never lost his footing to throw his rider, and never failed when needed to make a river crossing, even in icy and treacherous water.

The horseman's last tribute was with understandable feeling: "Farewell, gallant old friend. May the turf on the banks of the Highwood lie lightly over you."

15

Duke

Instincts of a Homing Pigeon

William Lauder's red-roan gelding did not like the Yukon. Homesick for the Nicola Valley in southern British Columbia where he was raised, he was determined to return. Demonstrating some of the qualities of a homing pigeon, the aging horse made his way through hundreds of miles of unbroken wilderness, making no mistake in directions. It must have been one of the most remarkable equine feats on record.

Stories have been written about dogs and cats using their hidden resources to guide them through unfamiliar territory to what they considered their home ground. But where, if ever, was there a homing adventure to rival that of the Lauder horse, beginning at Dawson City in the Yukon and ending in southern British Columbia? Fortunately, Joe Lauder

74

of Springbank Ranch, Quilchena, could recall the circumstances as his father related them.

While modern man enthuses about the spectacular advances in science and technology, he should be reminded of the still greater wonders in the realms of nature — the inner workings of animal bodies, for example, the complexities of reproduction, the undefinable mysteries of instinct which guides birds in migration and horses and dogs trying to return to home quarters.

Joe Lauder represented the third generation of his family to occupy Springbank Ranch, near Douglas Lake. There, the grandfather settled in 1876, long before the first railway had penetrated the province. Continuously, the ranch produced cattle and horses. But to William Lauder there was something special about the roan gelding known as Duke because it gave him his first exercise in branding. It was just after his return from school in Ontario in 1886, and the brand was "JL" on the left shoulder. Both the event and the young horse stood out clearly in his memory.

When Duke became three years of age, he was broken to saddle and, thereafter, he was used for general riding around the ranch. He was soon recognized as one of the better stock horses, with speed and agility and wind. These characteristics, along with a distinctive color, made Duke a source of pride to the cowboy riding him. The same qualities would make him attractive to horse thieves and one day, early in 1898, Duke was missing. At first, nobody took much notice of the horse's disappearance, it being supposed that he had found some good grazing in a remote part of the big ranch. "He'll wander back in his own good time," the riders reasoned.

But Duke did not wander back as expected. William Lauder began to suspect theft and notified the mounted police. The law officers responded at once, but because of the lapse of time after the animal's disappearance, they were working under a handicap. Everybody agreed that a red-roan horse with the JL brand on his left shoulder would be easy enough to identify. The probability was that the thief of an easily recognizable animal would choose to take it far away. The problem would be in overtaking Duke.

As there was no longer any doubt about the horse having been stolen, the officers continued their search. Men at the Lauder ranch were angry about having one of their best horses whisked away but they admitted that the culprit knew a good beast when he saw one.

Police obtained some leads and traced the stolen horse to Vancouver where it had been loaded on a boat and shipped to Skagway, Alaska. The gold rush to the diggings near Dawson City in the Yukon was gaining momentum. Most of the eager prospectors were attempting to reach the mines by way of Skagway and the treacherous Chilkoot route. There were mountain passes, terrible gorges and dangerous water courses. Pack horses were needed and it was easy to suppose that the Lauder gelding had been sent north for that purpose.

As time was to show quite horribly, most of the horses that started with packs and loads from Skagway died along the trail. Some were buried when struck by an avalanche from a mountain side; some lost footing on narrow ledges and plunged to their death, and some collapsed from sheer exhaustion. It was a cruel adventure for horses but a few of the hardy ones successfully negotiated the passes and the rocky trails and rode rafts through the wild White Horse rapids to arrive safely at Dawson City.

Police studies showed that the Lauder gelding was one of those to reach that remote center of mining madness. But before the officers could overtake the animal and ascertain who had taken it from the British Columbia ranch, it disappeared again. It was not difficult to conclude that the emaciated horse had simply strayed away to die or had been killed by wolves or bears. Nobody at Dawson City would be greatly concerned. The job for which the animal was wanted had been completed and no miner would care to buy hay at forty or fifty dollars per bale to feed a horse he did not need. Dawson City in those gold-rush years would be an inhospitable place for a horse and Duke was smart enough to realize it.

A year went by and then two years. The Lauders abandoned all hope of seeing their roan horse again. It could be assumed that the bones of the lamented Duke were scattered with those of other unfortunate horses along the trails out of Skagway. To their astonishment, however, the Lauders received a rumor about a roan gelding carrying the JL brand on its left shoulder being seen traveling south on the Cariboo Trail. It seemed impossible that the horse heading toward Kamloops and Douglas Lake could be the one stolen from the ranch two years previously, but they investigated and, sure enough, there was Duke — identified unmistakably by color and brand — on his way home to the ranch where he was raised.

There was a happy reunion between the sixteen-year-old horse and his rightful owners. Back on the Lauder range, Duke went to the pastures he had not forgotten. He seemed to know that his worries and hardships were over. He would have good grass and friendly associations as long as he lived.

The exact route followed from Dawson City to the settled parts of British Columbia would never be known. The Lauders considered the possibility that he came south by Teslin Lake, Telegraph Creek and Hazelton. These were points touched by Norman Lee when he made his historic and unsuccessful cattle drive in the direction of Dawson City in 1898. That the horse could get through at all seemed incredible. Where was he during two northern winters? How did he cross the big rivers along the way? How many times was his course blocked by mountains, necessitating wide detours? These and other questions would never be answered. His sense of direction must have been unerring, just as his judgment about where he would have a good home was faultless.

16

Old Buck

The Winnipeg Patriarch

Horses living to the age of 40 years are about as uncommon as men living to 125. The buckskin gelding known as Buck, 41 years of age at the time of his death in 1948, was believed to be the oldest horse in Canada at that time, perhaps the oldest on the continent. There was no pedigree certificate to make it official but private records showing place and date of birth were sufficient to remove all doubt. Buck was foaled on a farm at Maiden Rock, near Lake Pippin in Wisconsin, and his year was 1907.

Horsemen who visited the equine patriarch when he was forty years of age saw him as a dignified and friendly old gentleman. Naturally, the weight of years was telling. His joints were less nimble than in earlier years; he was becoming quite gray about the head and the bloom of youth had departed. But there remained an uncommon interest in his admiring guests — he seemed to understand as visitors talked about him and to him.

Great age was not his only mark of distinction because Buck had had an unusually active career. Nobody would call it a glamorous career; he had never been a show horse or circus horse or rodeo performer. Rather, he was a working horse but a specialist in his own field.

With his distinctive coat, Buck furnished support for the view expressed many times by pioneer farmers that "you can't kill a buckskin." Perchance there was a biological relationship between the buckskin color and reputed buckskin hardiness, just like the genetic relationship which appeared to exist between Appaloosa coat pattern and sparse hair in mane and tail. The Indians of the plains believed that buckskin horses possessed the best degree of stamina and farmers on the frontier agreed.

Anyway, Buck was typical of the strain, with yellowish hair, black mane and tail, and dark strip down the back and across the withers. In addition to those characteristics inherited from western mustang stock on his mother's side, Buck had grace of movement and sense of pride from improved English breeds on the paternal side of his pedigree.

For the first few years of his life, Buck was just another lightweight farm horse, expected to pull the family buggy in summer and the cutter in winter, help bring the cows home from the pasture at milking times and perform any other chores which might fall to a horse of his size and type.

At the age of eight years, the buckskin gelding was sold and taken to a big city. Probably he was unhappy in being separated from familiar stables and pastures. His new work was at the stockyards at South St. Paul and for the next four years he spent his working hours in carrying commission agents up and down the alleys, sorting beef animals and generally directing cattle traffic. In 1919, when thousands of settlers were coming into western Canada from the United States, Buck was among the immigrants. He was shipped to Winnipeg and taken to the Union Stockyards at St. Boniface where experienced horses were needed to carry stock saddles and work with cattle in the pens and alleys.

When he reached twelve years of age, Buck would have a "smooth mouth" and could have been considered as being "past his best." But he was still vigorous and, two years after coming to Canada, he was bought to work for the livestock commission firm of Weiller and Williams in the St. Boniface yards. Before long, he was accepted as one of the firm's most faithful servants. Year after year he carried commission men as they negotiated the long lanes at the busy stockyards. He became proficient; like an experienced hand, he entered into the work of sorting cattle until observers said he knew nearly as much about grading and grouping market stock as the human experts in the business. He understood the ways of cattle, could outguess an obstreperous cow trying to make her escape or deal a well-directed kick between the eyes of a vicious bull about to launch an attack.

It was Buck's good fortune, in coming to the Weiller and Williams firm, to become the direct responsibility of William McGugan, an understanding horseman and able stockman. The alignment was one to ensure thoughtful care as long as the horse was a part of the Weiller and Williams operation. At the great age of thirty years, it was decided that Buck

81

should be and would be retired — with benefit of security. Mr. McGugan knew a farmer west of Winnipeg, at whose place the old horse could live out his remaining days in peace and ease. At his age, Buck could not be expected to live much longer anyway. The farmer was consulted and agreed to take the horse. Men who were present had difficulty in restraining tears as Buck was led away from what had been his stockyard home for sixteen years.

A few years passed. There was no report about Buck. It was easy for busy men at the stockyards to forget about the horse or assume that all was well with him. But all was not well, and as Mr. McGugan, on a summer evening, drove through a Winnipeg suburb his eyes fell upon a boy riding a buckskin horse at a gallop. There was something strangely familiar about the animal and the man turned his car and drove to overtake it. Sure enough, here was Buck, thin, dirty, and showing signs of neglect. There was a moment of reunion as the horse pressed its muzzle against the man's face. McGugan felt the return of an old affection.

"Where did you get this horse?" McGugan inquired. "Who owns hims now? I want to talk to his owner."

The boy could provide only limited explanation. He had merely rented the horse from a near-by riding stable and knew nothing of previous owners. It was evident that the animal had been sold from the farm on which it had been placed for retirement and McGugan was angry as he set out to find the latest owner. At the riding stable, he learned that the horse had been bought from a farmer west of Winnipeg and was being kept for rental to anybody willing to pay a dollar an hour for the privilege of a ride. McGugan became instantly determined to repossess the horse and asked: "How much will you take for him right now?" The stable owner confessed to the horse's advanced age and then named his price — thirty-five dollars. McGugan wrote a cheque for the amount and instructed that his old friend be delivered back at the stockyards where he had lived for so many years.

Buck, by this time thirty-five years old, walked into his former pen with all the confidence of ownership. He was back where the oats and hay and care had always been of the best. If horses pray, it seemed pretty evident that this old horse's prayers had been answered.

But Buck's adventures were not over. He was a horse with a reputation and when Winnipeg was organizing a spring horse show in May, 1946, men responsible for attractions were anxious to place the thirty-nine-year-old on public display. Buck did not fancy the idea but he was trucked to the stables at the show grounds and treated as a special guest. After much grooming and polishing and the gift of a new halter, he was led into the big ring to be greeted by 5,000 show patrons who cheered as they might have been expected to do for a visiting dignitary.

A show horse might have enjoyed the demonstration but Buck was unimpressed. He was one whose life had been given to useful work and he could not bring himself to enthusiasm for the bright lights. He was anxious to get away and did manage to get away. Soon after being returned to his stall in the show stable, he slipped the halter from his head and made his way out into the night. He was miles from his home quarters but he thought he knew how to get there.

As soon as the empty stall was noticed, anxious men set out to find the horse. Those who presumed that his instinct would take him unerringly toward his own box stall were right and they overtook him moving quickly through city streets he had never seen before, trying to determine the shortest route to the stockyards and home.

It should have been easy to guess Buck's thoughts: "Horse shows may be all right for giddy young horses but when one gets to be my age, nothing looks better than my own box stall and a manger filled with timothy hay such as my friends provide." This time, Buck was back home to enjoy his retirement without interruption until he died there at the very ripe age of forty-one years.

17

Delia D

The Captain's Dream Horse

Captain Stanley Harrison, who farmed near Fort Qu'Appelle, had a kindly feeling for birds, animals, flowers and all the wonderful things in nature's complex community, also the delightful ability to set those feelings to poetry. His special fondness, however, was for a good Thoroughbred horse with spirit and speed, and over the years, he raised some outstanding race track performers, like Chiron, Brockington and Torpedo. But which of all the horses he had owned remained closest to his heart? It was not an easy question for him because he loved them all. He would have to consider. There was his famous stallion, Pensweep, which inspired some of the lovely lines in Harrison's book, *Gentlemen, The Horse!* There was his faithful cavalry horse shot from under his saddle in World War I.

Then, there was Bendy, a mare about which Harrison wrote as an old and very dear friend: "Oh, Bendy, yes, a lovely mare with the heart of a fighter. She was swift and kind and belonged to the Delia D family too. She taught me that one must love a Thoroughbred, not for what it does in the eyes of the world, but for what it is in itself. She won three races in three starts and then fell on the track and broke a leg. They would have shot her but a gardener's wife who had fed her carrots, intervened, shielding the filly's frightened eyes from the gun and begged to give her a chance to recover. Bendy went to hospital and after six months she was all right except for one short leg and a stiff pastern. She was through racing but Bendy might have a career as a family mare. At first she was dogged by ill luck: dead twins, a dead single and then twins again. But her luck changed and she gave us five winners in a row. When Bendy grew old, we were not just man and horse; we were old friends."

It was the beautiful sentiment of a man with a genuine love for horses and a sensitive feeling for all God's creatures. But there was still another Thoroughbred candidate for the spot closest to the Harrison heart. She was Delia D, the Captain's Dream Horse, one of the first to capture the distinguished horseman's affection and one who transmitted her great spirit to racing offspring.

Between Harrison and Delia D, it was love at first sight. The moment of meeting was at Regina in 1911. Harrison and a friend sat in conversation in the rotunda of the King's Hotel. The talk was probably about horses. Whatever the subject, they were paying only the slightest attention to passing traffic, mainly horse-drawn drays, wagons and buggies. But suddenly, Harrison was distracted. His speech failed. As he stared anxiously through the window, his friend inquired: "What's wrong? Something bothering you?"

Harrison, still gazing intently into the street, replied: "Nothing is bothering me but didn't you notice the off mare in the buggy team that just went by? She looked every inch a Thoroughbred. Excuse me, I must overtake her, see if she's for sale. Good-bye."

Harrison streaked from the hotel and down the street as if being chased by a bull. Fortunately, the owner of the team had stopped at the post office and was tying to the hitching post when Harrison reached the place. Out of breath, he studied the mare and the second impression was even more favorable than the first. There she stood, his Dream Horse, a rich chestnut, 16 hands high, alert and proud in her bearing and magnificent in quality. He admired the character in her head, the muscling in her back and quarters, the flintiness in her clean hocks, the flatness of her shanks and refinement of pasterns.

Answers to Harrison's eager questions indicated that she was, indeed, a Thoroughbred, foaled in Kentucky. He tried to hide his enthusiasm but his heart was beating rapidly and he was already determined to have her. The owner was reluctant but he confessed that he needed money and would part with her for $175. Harrison did not have that much and did not know where he could get it but he paid five dollars as a deposit and promised to pay the balance before the end of the day.

Delia D went to her new home where she won admiration and good care. More than ever, Harrison was finding something fine and cultural in good horses. "The story of the horse," he said, "is the

story of civilization.'' Then he repeated the idea in
verse:

    Clear through the song of history throbs the beat
    Of swift and dauntless hoofs in thunderous flight,
    To wrest some epic victory from defeat
    And turn the darkness of despair to light.

Came World War I and Stanley Harrison responded to the call. His absence demanded major
adjustments on the farm and Delia D was placed in
the care of the owner's brother. She produced a foal
and toward war's end, soon to foal again, she strayed
from the home farm. Some months elapsed and she
was presumed to have been stolen or to have died.

Home to recuperate after a series of war wounds,
Harrison received the news of Delia's disappearance
with deep sorrow. He was accepting his loss
philosophically until he heard about a stray chestnut
mare meeting Delia's description seen about fifteen
miles from the home farm. The rest of the story was
disturbing: the mare had died beside a strawpile in an
unfenced field, leaving an orphan foal of two or three
tender months.

Harrison lost no time in conducting an investigation. He found the strawpile, found the remains of a
horse whose bones had been picked clean by
coyotes, found a half-starved filly foal almost dead
on her feet. With emotion he could not hide, he
talked with neighbors and learned of their amazement at the foal's survival. They described the mare
as a 16-hands chestnut with fine Thoroughbred
characteristics and told about the young foal, suddenly deprived of milk and forced to forage for a
living. Tears probably came to Harrison's eyes
when he heard about the stunted foal wandering up to
a mile from the strawpile each day in search of some

tender feed and returning each night to lie beside the bones of its mother.

There was no doubt; the bones were those of Harrison's beloved Delia D and the foal was his property. The neighbors, who had watched the baby becoming more like a walking skeleton every day, were inclined to apologize for their failure to destroy the wee thing and thus end its misery. But the very suggestion of shooting Delia's foal filled Harrison with anger. The very idea! Kill Delia's baby which had done so valiantly to survive? Never. He would do all in his power to see that the baby had a chance to mature, even if it was a runty specimen in which no other person could see any good. Hastening home, he constructed a stoneboat for transporting the foal and in another day, the orphan was enjoying the luxury of a box stall and the most nourishing feed the Stockwell Farm could provide.

Instead of dying, the filly grew strong and active and was given a name, Redwing. She might never be big and beautiful like her mother but she gave assurance of having the mother's courage and quality and Harrison was happy to have a means of perpetuating the Delia D line. Redwing was allowed to run with her older brother, Merry Marquis, and they became staunch pals. At three years of age, the filly was having a foal. It was too early for a stunted mother but the fact had to be accepted and the wobbly new baby was called Dusky.

Like other members of her family, Dusky possessed pronounced individuality. Stanley Harrison recognized it and saw her as a Thoroughbred with a future in racing. Renamed Merry Minx, she was out as a two-year-old and won futurity races at Calgary and Edmonton. Having inherited the unbeatable spirit of her mother and grandmother, she continued to prove her metal and won racing honors on Canadian and United States tracks. When Harrison shipped a string of fourteen Thoroughbreds to race in the United States and then in Cuba, his horses were struck by a virulent fever and all but four died. Merry Minx was one of the survivors. Later, after racing at Calgary where the mare was a winner, the Harrison horses were on their way to a meet in Winnipeg when their freight car was involved in a wreck. At first it appeared that all the horses had been killed but when some of the wreckage was cleared away, Merry Minx emerged bruised and bleeding but very much alive. And, at Winnipeg, just a few days later, she won her race. Such was the stuff that was in this granddaughter of Delia D. "She was true and game and I loved her for it," said Captain Stanley Harrison. She was a worthy daughter of the orphaned Redwing, the worthy granddaughter of the Captain's Dream Horse.

18

Grattan Bars

Wonder Horse of 1928

As long as horsemen have memories, they will be talking about the Standardbred pacing stallion, Grattan Bars. They will concede something about his disposition leaving much to be desired and then argue that no pacer in the world could have passed him when he made up his mind to go. He was one of the first Canadian-bred horses to pace a mile in less than two minutes. The wonder horse of his time, his rise to fame was like that of the ugly duckling which outgrew its misfortunes and became a beautiful swan.

As a colt, Grattan Bars was rough and unattractive. Nobody could see much future for him, and when he changed hands as a yearling, the payment consisted of two calves and two young pigs — in other words, less than a hundred dollars' worth of farm livestock. But there came the day when, with a proud racing record, the great Standardbred was attracting offers running into six figures.

Canadian horsemen found reason for interest in various members of Grattan Bars' family, especially in his father, Grattan Royal, another "rags-to-riches horse." There was nothing dull about the Grattans. They lived dangerously and lived dramatically. Grattan Royal, a big bay horse with three white feet, rose from obscurity to fame, not once but twice. Bred in Illinois, he was purchased and brought to Canada by Charles Barrett, of Park Hill, Ontario. He was raced successfully in Canada and then on the American Grand Circuit, making a time record for a mile of 2:06¼. But racing was always attended by risks in many forms and Grattan Royal had his misfortunes. After changing owners a time or two, he became lame, and when the condition appeared to be permanent, he was retired to a farm in Iowa.

It has happened many times that a man or a horse has held the public gaze as long as he was winning but when misfortune overtook him, he was forgotten quickly. Grattan Royal was the forgotten horse — at least until his Canadian offspring became old enough to show the superior racing ability they had inherited from their father. Charles Barrett, who had owned him in Canada, was the first to recognize this special quality in the young horses and resolved to find the old sire and bring him back to Canada.

Locating an aging and almost forgotten stallion in the big area represented by the United States proved difficult, but Barrett was determined. "If the old fellow is still alive," the Ontario man was saying to himself, "I'm going to find him and own him again." His investigations led to the Central States and finally, after using the advertising columns of the press, he succeeded in finding Grattan Royal on the Iowa farm.

The old horse was still very lame and showing signs of neglect. He was thin; his coat was dry and harsh and his feet were overgrown from lack of attention. Even after studying the horse and noting the white star on his forehead, Barrett was not sure the horse at which he was looking was really Grattan Royal. What finally confirmed identity to his satisfaction was a peculiar small lump on the horse's tail. Barrett was able to buy the horse for $200 and took immediate possession of him. Back at his original Canadian home, the old stallion regained some of his former spirit and remained there until his death in 1924, at the age of seventeen years.

In the meantime, sons and daughters were winning more races and winning attention. And, as revealed later, the most famous son was Grattan Bars, a bay with three white feet and a star on his forehead. His breeder and original owner was Archie Pedden, of Strathroy, Ontario, and his birth date was May 15, 1923. Thus, Grattan Bars was only one year old when his father died.

No doubt his mother, a mare called Polly Bars, thought her baby was wonderful but there was not much evidence of human enthusiasm. The colt's second owner was Fred Thrower, Kerrwood, Ontario, and he had the difficult task of breaking and training this youngster with a noticeable wild streak in him. Patience was needed, but the son of Polly Bars was soon to show encouraging signs of speed as well as the discouraging traces of rebellion in his disposition. Optimism has always been a characteristic of men in the racing fraternity and Thrower believed he would have a great pacer if only the fierce personality could be subdued.

Grattan Bars was always a difficult horse to handle on the track. His drivers were known to say that their job was like handling a bull moose in harness. But how he could pace when he wanted to do it! He had stamina and coordination to please the most fastidious judges and his mark of 1:59½ for the mile gained world praise. Horsemen wondered how much faster he could have traveled if he had been subjected to earlier and more intensive training. An American horseman who had watched racing for many years gave it as his opinion that Grattan Bars had more potential for racing than any other pacer in North American history.

But his racing career was a short one. As a three-year-old with limited training, he started in only one race; it was at Toronto and he won all three heats. In his four-year-old form, 1927, he was entered in eleven Ontario races and won them all. And in 1928, his big year, he was matched against some of the best United States horses and continued to distinguish himself. Among the successes on United States tracks in that season were three $25,000 stakes won in a period of two weeks and climaxed by the winning of the American Pacing Derby at Kalamazoo. Clearly, he was the pacing sensation of the year. And Canadians could not overlook the fact that Grattan Bars' strongest competition on the United States tracks was coming from another Canadian horse, one bearing the good name of Winnipeg.

Canadian horsemen were very proud and the horse's owner had the satisfaction of meeting many people who wanted to buy him. Writing from his farm at Kerrwood on February 22, 1930, Mr. Thrower admitted that Grattan Bars could be bought but wanted interested parties to be under no illusions about the probable cost and mentioned having refused "$100,000 three times one afternoon."

The year of 1928 marked not only the great horse's peak in performance but also his last racing year. Suffering from a new physical handicap in the autumn of that year, he was retired to the Ontario farm. But for the Grattans, the stream of life never flowed smoothly and in a few years, Grattan Bars was involved in a ferocious fight with another stallion and suffered injuries which led to the necessity of destroying him, the wonder horse of Canadian Standardbred racing up to that time. It was a serious loss to the breed. But Canadian horsemen could not forget their delight at his great performance record. "Sure he was roughneck," said one elderly horseman, "but he was the greatest thing that ever hit the race track."

19

Wee Donald

Every Inch a Champion

Some farm horses were unlucky in the humans who claimed and used them, and suffered ill treatment as a consequence. Some were lucky in being owned by kindly and considerate people. A few were especially lucky, like Wee Donald, the big Clydesdale stallion whose admiring and devoted owner was Charles Weaver, of the Lloydminster district. And in return for good care and affection dispensed lavishly, the horse brought international honors to the Weavers on three occasions.

Next to Seager Wheeler's succession of world championships for wheat, nothing brought more pride to prairie people than the three championships won by Wee Donald at the International Fat Stock Shows at Chicago in 1920, 1921 and 1924. No other Canadian horse gained such a championship record

at Chicago although other Canadian Clydesdale
stallions added to the Canadian record: First Principal, owned by the Manitoba Department of Agriculture, was the international champion in 1922; Main-
ring, owned by W. B. Cleland, Troy, Ontario, was
the Chicago champion in 1923; Green Meadow
Footstep, owned by the University of Saskatchewan, was champion in 1925; Forest Favorite, owned
by Haggerty and Black, Belle Plain, was champion in
1926; Sansovina, for John Sinclair of Congress,
Saskatchewan, was the 1927 champion; Lochinvar
won it for John Falconer of Govan, Saskatchewan,
in 1928. and Sonny Boy won it for A. Johnstone, of
Yellowgrass, also in Saskatchewan, in 1929. Thus,
Canadian Clydesdale stallions won the high international honor for ten consecutive years. But only
Wee Donald won it three times.

Wee Donald was bred by R. D. Ferguson, Port
Stanley, Ontario, and foaled on May 17, 1914. He
had a brown coat, white face and four white "stockings," also a stylish pedigree, as any Clydesdale
fancier would agree. His father was Hugo's Stamp
and back of him was a succession of horses with great
names: Sir Hugo, Sir Everard, Top Gallant, and that
cornerstone of the breed, Darnley.

Vanstone and Rogers, of North Battleford,
bought Wee Donald and brought him to the West as a
two-year-old. It was a time when the prairie country
needed working horses, breeding horses, any kind of
horses, in large numbers. The demand seemed almost unlimited. Vanstone and Rogers were among
the horse dealers who were bringing thousands of
head from the East, from the United States and from
beyond the Atlantic. The Scottish Clydesdale was
still the favored breed and showring competitions
were marked by the same sort of zeal that was

brought to national elections. In his first year in the West, Wee Donald was exhibited at the Saskatoon Exhibition but did not attract special attention. Shown as a three-year-old in the next season, he was catching the eyes of judges and others and, at both Saskatoon and Regina exhibitions, he won his classes and the reserve championship for Canadian-bred Clydesdale stallions.

Charlie Weaver, a Lancashire man who in 1906 homesteaded on the west side of the Alberta-Saskatchewan meridian, nine miles north of Lloyd-minster, was looking for a stallion. Seeing the Vanstone and Rogers horse, he was convinced at once that this was the one for him. Weighing close to a ton, Wee Donald had a muscular body, flat bone in his limbs, clean and hard hocks, sloping pasterns, broad feet to give him a "good grip o' the ground," and the ability to move with a bold and straight stride and clocklike flection of leg joints. He seemed proud to belong to the old Scottish breed.

With Weaver as his new owner, Wee Donald was out at the spring shows in 1920 and won the Canadian-bred championships for Clydesdale stallions at Regina and Edmonton. It was then that the suggestion about showing at Chicago was advanced. Weaver was game to test his horse in the "Big League" and Wee Donald was fitted and sent forward. And to justify his owner's faith, the horse won the championship for the breed. After repeating in 1921 and 1924, Weaver was sure he had the greatest horse in the world.

Charlie Weaver was showman as well as owner. He spent hundreds of hours grooming and training his big pet. He could tie up a tail and roll a mane like an expert, always finishing these operations with gold and purple ribbons, "Wee Donald's colors."

And, then, having prepared the big horse for the showring, Weaver always hoped for music because Wee Donald loved it and would prance to it, thereby capturing the attention of judge and spectators. For purposes of parades which so often followed competitions, Weaver had a white satin collar fitted to Donald's neck for the display of medals.

By the time Wee Donald was winning international championships, nothing was too good for him. Weaver built him a private barn, small but big enough and attractive. Across it was painted in big letters: "Wee Donald's House." Back of this private dwelling was a grassy field, exclusively Donald's. When most horses were eating only hay or straw, Donald was receiving rations of oats and bran with appetizers of sugar and molasses.

He liked fresh bread, especially the kind made in Mrs. Weaver's kitchen, and managed to get generous allowances of it. When a loaf of fresh bread disappeared from the pantry, Mrs. Weaver knew where it had gone. She could recall, also, the loss of certain household utensils and would ultimately find them at Wee Donald's House. "I've lost my scissors," she would say and Charlie Weaver would be obliged to confess that he had them down at Donald's House to do some trimming and forgot to bring them back. When she bought a new bread-mixer with handle on the top, it, too, disappeared. Where was it discovered? In Donald's House where the utensil's merit for mixing Wee Donald's feed was under consideration.

If the horse enjoyed the company of a loyal human with a Lancashire accent, he should have been satisfied, because he had a lot of it. When anybody inquired: "Where is Mr. Weaver?" or "Where is Dad?" the answer was nearly always the same: "He's down at Donald's House." When Miriam Green Ellis, Western Editor of the *Family Herald and Weekly Star*, traveled to Lloydminster to see Wee Donald and interview Mr. Weaver, she found him in the horse's box stall, gazing in admiration as the big horse masticated his oats. "You seem to like Wee Donald a good deal," she commented, to which he replied: "That I do. He's good company. It's many a pipe of tobacco I've smoked just sitting here in his stall and admiring those grand feet and legs." Then, after a brief pause, he added: "You know, he's my friend and there isn't enough money in all the world to buy him from me. I'll never part with Donald."

But it was only a short time until tragedy struck. It was harvest time and Donald, feeling frisky, broke from the boy who was leading him to water. Running toward some other horses, he tried to jump a fence and fell and broke his back. Although nursed with all the care Charlie Weaver could supply, he died soon after and was buried on the farm. It was, indeed, the loss of a dear friend, of something more precious than money as the man had pointed out: "There isn't enough money in all the world to buy him from me."

20

Adounad

An Arabian Pioneer

For many British Columbia horsemen, Adounad was the first representative of his breed they had ever seen. If he was not the first purebred Arabian in that province which was destined to become a breed stronghold, he was one of the first and when the Canadian Arabian Horse Stud Book, Volume One, was published, Adounad's registration number was "5." Perhaps it should have been "1" because Adounad was on the Canadian scene some years ahead of the four horses with lower numbers. And in bringing the breed to the attention of British Columbia people, Adounad was the outstanding pioneer.

"The last time I saw Adounad," a horseman wrote, "was in the showring at Kelowna. At the age of 23 or 24 years, some of his former bloom had departed and the old timer didn't win his class but he appeared like the Elder Statesman, looking condescendingly at the noisy and giddy young stallions around him." A short time later, at the age of 26, death came to the grand old horse and tears came to the eyes of some British Columbia horse lovers.

His advanced age was further evidence of Arabian longevity. A few Canadian horsemen could recall seeing Adounad's sire, Hanad, at Mrs. Alice Payne's place in California, when 27 years of age and sharing stable facilities with the 28-year-old Arabian mare, Poka; the 23-year-old desert-bred mare, Aziza, with foal at foot; the 26-year-old Raseyn, son of the celebrated Skowronek, and the 23-year-old Raffles, also a son of Skowronek. It was a notable collection of senior citizens of the Arabian Horse Community.

Adounad was an aristocrat and seemed to be conscious of it. And why not? Did he not belong to the oldest breed of improved livestock in the world? Were his ancestors not the most prized possessions of Sheiks traveling the deserts of Arabia for a thousand years? Did the Arabian horse stock not furnish the foundation upon which the English Thoroughbred was built and the means of improving a score of other breeds? The Arabian horses were late in coming to Canada but when they did come, their acceptance was rapid, even spectacular. Like every good horse of the ancient breed, Adounad held his head high, carried his tail with a gay flourish and stepped with unmistakable pride. His back was short and his loins and croup were well muscled. He was an Arabian and left no doubt about it.

This son of Hanad was bred by the Kellogg Ranch in California, foaled April 6, 1931, and registered as a bay with a small star on his forehead and white on his off hind foot. As a yearling, he was

imported to Canada by Charles J. Taylor, of Vancouver. He changed hands again and then came into
the ownership of Mr. and Mrs. C. S. Latimer, of
Chilliwack — later Vernon. While owned by the
Latimers, Adounad gained fame and exerted an unusual influence. Among his offspring were many of
the best Anglo-Arabs seen in Canadian showrings.

The Latimers, with sentiment becoming to true
horsemen, revered the day Adounad came into their
possession. For the stallion, it was no less a day of
good fortune although sickness at the time made it
difficult for anybody to be optimistic about the
animal's future. The point was that Adounad arrived
at his new home suffering from what may have been
shipping fever. Whatever the condition, it was severe. He did not look like a horse which would stay
around for another seventeen years.

"We bought him in the fall of 1940," Mrs.
Latimer recalled, "and his journey from the Island in
the worst of November weather brought him to us
with a shocking cold. We wondered if we were going
to save him. And so, right from the beginning, we
learned what a courageous fellow he was. He dis-
liked being fussed over but he had to put up with
much nursing." The weeks of intensive care brought
their special reward, well worth the anxiety, as Mrs.
Latimer said, "for the three of us came to know each
other very well indeed."

After that initial setback, the stout-hearted
Adounad was "never sick or sorry" until old age
began to have its effect. He was always ready for a
canter across the fields or a trip to a horse show. His
personality was constantly brilliant and, again in
Mrs. Latimer's words, "anything written about him
would have to be as honest and direct as he was."

Friendliness came as naturally as eating hay and

early in his life he seemed to develop a sense of responsibility for the welfare of people and horses around him. Everything at Orchardcroft Farm had his attention. "When we first came to Vernon in 1943," Mrs. Latimer wrote, "we had stabling right in town and I often rode Adounad on one of the main streets while leading a mare and letting her foal run by her side. Sometimes we would go to the open country and then, when the foal would take liberties and gambol far from its mother's side, it was Adounad who called the baby back, not its mother. He was always gentle with young things and small, whether foals or children or dogs. The dog we had then became his constant companion and travelled with him when we went to shows, staying in Adounad's box stall. They grew old together, those two."

And while attempting to define his personality, Mrs. Latimer recalled one of the few times when exasperation overcame his customary patience. Having reached the age of twenty-three years, he knew he was entitled to respect from all, certainly from his own offspring. "His Anglo-Arab son, Fargo, was just five, justifiably proud of himself and not above showing it. Adounad had his own paddock, with a lane up to it from the stable and closed from the stable yard by a gate at the bottom. Fargo was allowed his freedom in the yard after exercise for a while daily and, soon, we noticed him choosing to stand in front of Adounad's lane gate. It appeared to annoy our old boy considerably. We tried to stop the young horse's impudent conduct but one day when everyone's attention was elsewhere, Fargo resumed his stand in front of the gate that Adounad considered his own. The old horse was displeased and resolved to do something about it. He trotted to the end of the lane, looked over the gate as if to issue one last warning, laid his ears back and, like a blast from a cannon, shot through the closed gate, much to Fargo's surprise and horror. The younger horse streaked to his own box with Adounad right on his heels but once the young one had been sent home, Adounad simply turned and walked back to his paddock. He had no further problem with his son.''

The record of Adounad's winnings in both halter and saddle classes would entail much space and the list of successes of sons and daughters would be even longer. Mention has been made of Fargo, whose mother was a Thoroughbred, one of the outstanding hacks in the history of Canadian shows. He was tall, graceful, refined, and possessed feet and legs which seemed well-nigh perfect. His championships were many and he had half-brothers and half-sisters with similar records of showring success.

The Adounad influence upon Arabian and half-bred horses for pleasure and show was supremely high. That much was acknowledged. But in addition, there was the Adounad who made people love him. Those who knew him in his later years would remember him as a kindly and understanding old gentleman, one with the marks of a loyal friend.

21

Blanche Kesako

The Model Mare

History tells of one of the founding stallions in the Thoroughbred breed being "discovered" performing the menial task of pulling a water cart on the streets of Paris about the year 1724. When the horse's superior type and quality were recognized, it was bought and sent to England. There it was presented to Lord Godolphin and given the name Godolphin Barb. And there the stallion lived to the age of twenty-nine, gaining fame with every passing year. Ultimately, Godolphin Barb was recognized as one of three stallions and forty mares imported at the time of King Charles II, which provided the foundation for the English Thoroughbred.

The Canadian Percheron mare, Blanche Kesako, came too late to be part of her breed's beginning but her "discovery" on an out-of-the-way country trail in Saskatchewan was similar to that of Godolphin Barb, and no less romantic. Although slow in winning attention, Blanche—like Godolphin Barb—was an immediate sensation, especially in the Percheron showring.

Foaled in 1918, Blanche Kesako was raised by H. W. Belle, of Meyronne, Saskatchewan. Mr. Belle had good horses but they were not well known beyond the home community and Blanche, for the first ten years of her life, was never in a major showring and never far from her birthplace. Nobody had ever seen her in show condition and probably nobody would ever have seen her at her best had it not been for the keen eye of one of Western Canada's most memorable and stubborn and dedicated horsemen, Charles M. Rear.

Rear was an individualist, an eccentric, one whose conversation, thought and life were ruled almost entirely by his interest in horses, Percherons in particular. He imported and sold hundreds of stallions and was ready at any moment to buy, sell or trade.

He might be absent-minded and sometimes gave the impression of complete detachment from the world around him, but in judging horses and in buying and selling, he rarely made mistakes.

This was the man who when driving his Ford car on a country road in southern Saskatchewan in 1927 met a stubborn farmer driving a team of gray horses hitched to a wagonload of lumber. The man on the wagon was showing a horseman's fine scorn for motor vehicles; instead of pulling over to yield half the road to the car driver, he kept to the center and forced the motorist to drive into the ditch in order to pass. Charlie Rear at the wheel of his car was annoyed and allowed his vehicle to stop in the ditch so

107

that he might give the teamster a piece of his mind. Anger showed in Rear's eyes but he had never been too angry or too busy or too rushed to notice a good horse, and before he was in a position to speak, he caught a glimpse of the big gray mare on the near side, and became instantly speechless. He forgot about being angry and when he could speak he sputtered some questions: "Where did this mare come from?" "Is she purebred?" "How old is she?" "Will you sell her?"

The driver was flattered that a stranger would be impressed and answered the questions, one by one. The mare was raised right in that area; she was purebred and registered as Blanche Kesako in the Canadian Percheron Stud Book; she was nine years old and not for sale.

The last answer was disappointing but Rear gazed admiringly at the mare's great shoulders and short back and heavy muscling. Best of all, she had the refinement of feet and hoofheads and pasterns and cannon bones and hocks which would fill even a breeder of Clydesdales with delight.

"What a mare!" he was muttering to himself. "What a pity she is not for sale. But I have to own her sometime."

When he could not buy her on the spot, he left instructions that when she was for sale, he would be notified. He vowed again that he would own that mare.

A year passed and in the autumn of 1928 it was announced that the mare's owner was having an auction sale. Blanche Kesako would be among the animals offered. The date was in conflict with some of Rear's other plans, and when it appeared that he could not be present for the sale, he instructed his cousin, Leslie Foster, living near Kincaid, to attend

108

and buy the mare. The sum of $530 was forwarded for the purchase and if more were needed, it too would be supplied. Then, after furnishing buying instructions, Rear found that he could change the earlier plans and be at the sale to do his own bidding. He bought Blanche and her unregistered teammate for $410, and almost immediately sold the unregistered animal for $200, leaving Blanche in his ownership at a net cost of $210.

Rear was elated, as he should have been. He was sure his new mare had what she needed to be a champion. "It's too bad you couldn't have shown her at this year's Royal Winter Fair in Toronto," one of Rear's friends said, "but it's too late now; the entries have closed and the Saskatchewan Exhibits have already gone forward by freight. It is unfortunate."

Rear responded with a snicker: "Don't worry. She'll be there. She's entered already and I'll have her there."

It was then revealed that the resourceful Charlie Rear, intent upon owning the mare and confident of her quality, had acted weeks before the auction sale and actually entered Blanche Kesako in the classes at the Royal, in his own name as owner. And to get her there in time for the show, he had arranged to ship her by express instead of the usual freight. Shipping a horse weighing nearly a ton was costly and the mare, which had rarely spent a day or a night away from the home farm, did not like the experience. Traveling alone, she was very much upset and at Winnipeg it was thought necessary to call a veterinarian to attend her. Her disorder was diagnosed as simple homesickness and nothing could be prescribed to cure it.

Arriving at Toronto, Blanche seemed to improve

Louis Welsh, clearing the seven-foot jump on Barra Lad, reputed to have been the greatest jumper in Canadian history.

Scroll in honor of Sandy, originally a polo pony, who served admirably in World War I, and ended his career as a hunter. The scroll hangs in the Officers' Lounge, Canadian Army Base, Edmonton. Courtesy Princess Patricia's Canadian Light Infantry.

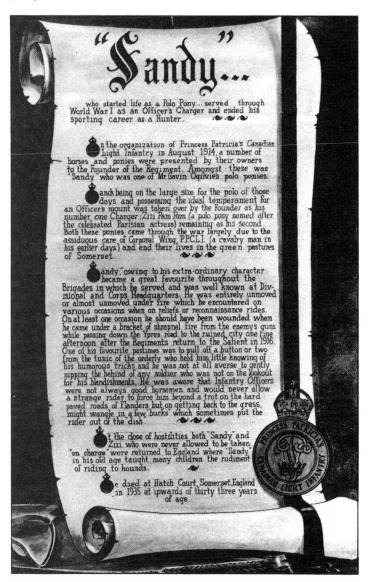

Old Buck in his fortieth year, January, 1947. At the time of his death in 1948, Buck was possibly the oldest horse on the North American continent.

Adounad, one of the first purebred Arabian stallions in Canada. Courtesy Mrs. Cliff Latimer.

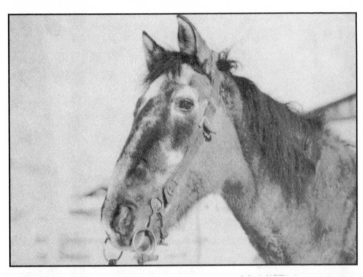

Clydesdales were the first of the work horse breeds to be widely accepted on Canadian farms. Here is the famous Clydesdale mare Langwater Jessica, mother of many champions, with her own and an adopted foal which she accepted after a little coaxing. Both filly foals went on to win awards at the Royal Winter Fair of 1930.

Brooms, the Thoroughbred stallion, whose proud character and gentle disposition endeared him to all who met him. October, 1944, at the University of Saskatchewan.

The Percheron mare Starlight Koncarness and her 1951 foal at the Salter farm near Calgary. Starlight, who began life as a lean, ungainly creature, was considered by many to have little promise as a show horse, but she went on to win forty-nine championships.

Burmese, a mare bred for the Royal Canadian Mounted Police, who became part of the internationally famous Musical Ride. She was presented to Her Majesty the Queen at Windsor Castle on April 28, 1969, the only Canadian horse ever to achieve that distinction. She is here ridden by Staff Sgt. R. Cave.

Justamere Stylish Stella, a Percheron mare who had one of the most notable showring careers in Canadian draft horse history. She was known to have gained as many as twenty-eight championships in a single year.

Bobbie, who gave twenty-two years of service to the Royal Canadian Mounted Police Musical Ride. He is here ridden by Constable R. Camm, a member of the 1953 Coronation Ride.

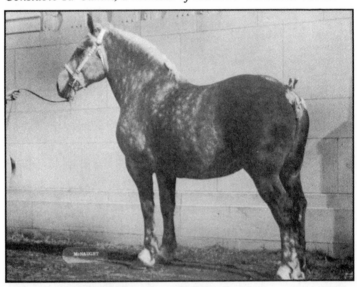

Rex Stonewall, the American Saddle Horse stallion, here ridden by Archie Currie. Rex lived a storybook life, from being mascot of a football team to barely escaping the slaughterhouse by falling into the clutches of thieves. Despite his many adventures, however, Rex managed to live out a peaceful retirement in the Burns and Company barn in east Calgary.

Kim's Kid, who entered the race as a long shot at twenty-five to one, wins the 1971 Canadian Derby at Northlands in Edmonton. He was ridden by Delbert Rycroft, shown below in the Winner's Circle. From inauspicious beginnings in a poor man's stable, Kim's Kid became the Wonder Horse of 1971.

but she was not fitted for high-class competition and her showring manners left much to be desired. But even without the customary preparation and her feet still showing neglect, Blanche stood fourth in the class for yeld mares and Rear was pleased. He promised that his green, country mare would return to win championships. Just a few days later he showed Blanche at the Ottawa Winter Fair and, sure enough, she won the grand championship for Percheron mares. It was her first championship but not her last.

While still the property of Mr. Rear, Blanche Kesako was shown at each of the next three Royal Winter Fairs, winning the reserve senior championship for mares of her breed in 1929, and grand championships in both 1930 and 1931. And while Blanche was the champion mare in those two latter years, Rear's gray stallion, Dean, was the grand champion male. During these years, too, Blanche was winning championships consistently at western exhibitions. She won the grand championship for mares at twelve major shows in 1929 alone, losing that high distinction on only one occasion.

Charlie Rear was a dealer and he surprised even himself in retaining Blanche for four years. But in 1932 he sold her to Carl Roberts, of Manitoba, owner of the stallion, Monarch, three times grand champion at the Canadian Royal Winter Fair. Exhibited by the new owner, the fifteen-year-old mare was reserve champion at the Royal in 1932 and soon thereafter was sold to go to Australia where she was hailed as the "Canadian sensation." A stallion foal born soon after her arrival in Australia proved to be a worthy son and the reports sent back led Carl Roberts to confess regret at having parted with the mare. "I would pay well for that stallion foal from old Monarch," he said.

Even after she was exported, horsemen were known to pronounce Blanche a near model of draft type. Farm Boys' Camp instructors liked to secure her for demonstration purposes and point to her superb shape. Some judges expressed the wish that she had more Percheron character in her head but nobody could fault her weight, which touched 2,250 pounds when fitted, a girth measurement reaching eight feet, three inches, an inspiring symmetry of body, depth at the chest, shortness of back, sloping shoulders, heavy muscling, an expansive spring of ribs, excellence of feet and legs, and the straight and true way of traveling at both walk and trot. Some observers said she was "just too good to be true," and marveled at how much the horse world would have missed if the team in which she was being driven in 1927 had not forced a certain Saskatchewan horseman off the road and into the ditch to fume in very temporary anger.

22

Langwater Jessica

Mother of Champions

If horse society offered an award for "The Mother Of The Year," the Clydesdale mare known as Langwater Jessica would have deserved it in 1930. Born, it seemed, to be a champion, the big roan mare with white face and feet and gentle disposition distinguished herself in various ways, first by winning championships in her own right, then by becoming the mother of champions, and finally in gaining recognition as a lovable old personality.

As a Clydesdale, she was, of course, a representative of the well-known draft breed developed in Scotland. Here was the first of the work horse breeds to be widely accepted on Canadian farms, mainly because many of the early settlers were Scottish and brought their preferences and loyalties in livestock with them. A good work horse, they reasoned, had to have more than the weight and muscle to move heavy loads and do it day after day. Scotland's horsemen had always demanded refinement and long-wearing qualities and although their Clydesdales were surpassed in size by Shires, Belgians and Percherons, they were unequalled in quality, especially in quality of feet and legs.

Jessica conformed to the best Scottish ideals in draft horse type, being in the weight range of 1,700 to 1,800 pounds and still refined and graceful. It meant that she and all typical representatives of the breed had clean-cut and flinty hocks, smooth and flat leg bones, long and sloping pasterns to furnish shock-absorbing benefits, big feet to allow added traction in doing field work, and finally, that straight and bold and stylish action marked by flection of joints and long strides.

Langwater Jessica was foaled in the United States in 1917, from a mare which had been previously owned in Alberta. After being bought by George A. Cluett, of Williamstown, Massachusetts, for $3,000, she was shown to win the reserve grand championship for Clydesdale mares at the International Fat Stock Show at Chicago on two occasions, once as a two-year-old in 1919 and again as a four-year-old in 1921. Soon after the latter showring success, Jessica was sold again, this time to become a Canadian, and from that time until her death in 1933, she was kept so busy raising foals that she had no time for the showring.

Jessica's Canadian home was at the University of Saskatchewan, Saskatoon, where horse breeding and improvement was a major undertaking at that time when farmers across the country depended almost entirely upon horses in the performance of field work. Dean W. J. Rutherford of the College of Agriculture was a lover of heavy horses, Clydesdales in particular, and as it happened, the money collected from insurance following the death of an imported stallion, Craigie Enchanter, was marked for investment in new Clydesdale stock. The result was that early in 1923, the University was able to buy the Cluett Clydesdales, thirteen head, including some of the aristocrats of the breed. Among the new horses to be stabled at Saskatoon were the stallion Kinleith Footprint, which had been a winner in Scotland before selling for $10,000; the mare Rosalind, which had won Scotland's highest showring honor in the Cawdor Cup; Craigie Sylvia, with two grand championships at Chicago to her credit; Langwater Jessica, and her first colt, a blue-roan to become famous as Green Meadow Footstep. The University was then the owner of one of the best groups of Clydesdales on the continent.

Jessica's first colt, Green Meadow Footstep, less than a year of age when he came to Saskatchewan, was big for his age and handsome. When he was three years old in 1925 he was shown at the Royal Winter Fair at Toronto and the International Show at Chicago and won the grand championship for stallions of his breed at both. It brought pride to western Canadian horsemen and brought fulfillment for one of Dean Rutherford's secret ambitions, to produce a Clydesdale stallion good enough to win an international championship.

When in show condition, Green Meadow Footstep weighed 2,400 pounds which would have to be regarded as heavy for any breed, and his successes brought added honor to Jessica. Best of all, this famous son of Jessica was not such an exception. Regularly every spring, about the time of the breakup on the South Saskatchewan River, the mare presented the University with a new foal and invariably it was a good one. One of them was Green Meadow Memory, a full sister to the big Footstep, and she in turn became a mother of champions.

But for great and motherly old Jessica, 1930 had to be the Banner Year of her life. On March 22, much as she had done year after year, the mare gave birth to a foal, this one a filly which was given the name of Julia. ''Another champion, no doubt,'' the visiting horsemen speculated. Mother and baby were both well. That was good but there was tragedy in the very next box stall; on the same date, the former International Grand Champion, Craigie Sylvia, died immediately after foaling, leaving a healthy filly foal which was later registered as Sylvia. The famous mare's death had to be accepted but what was to be done with the orphan which would never have the opportunity of tasting its own mother's milk?

Orphan foals can be raised by bottle feeding but the best efforts in artificial feeding have always been poor substitutes for mare's milk. The bottle-fed foal in almost every instance has been handicapped in its development. There was one possible alternative to a bottle-feeding plan: would old Jessica with a new foal condescend to accept the orphan along with her own baby and try to feed both? The danger in this proposal was that Jessica, with enough milk for one foal, would not have enough for two and both of the young and hungry things would suffer from underfeeding.

It was worth a trial. The orphan was brought into Jessica's box stall and she protested. She was a mare with a sweet disposition and had a great store of affection for her own baby, but did not want another one near her at this important moment in her private life. The horseman in charge knew that he had to be patient. Continuing to hold the orphan a safe distance from the mare, he talked to Jessica as if to explain the dilemma. Some of Jessica's own milk was smeared on the orphan's coat to make the baby smell more familiar and gradually the mare was getting the idea. Before the end of the day she had accepted the. double responsibility and the two hungry foals, one on each side, were nursing with delight.

At this point the mare demonstrated another hidden capacity, that of consuming unusually large amounts of feed and converting same to milk. Nobody had heard of such a thing before but Jessica's ration was increased until she was eating thirty-five pounds of a mixture of oats and bran per day — the equivalent of more than a bushel of oats — and manufacturing the milk needed to satisfy her two rapidly growing dependents. Not only did she feed them but she did what had never been done before; she fed them both well enough that both were ready for the showring at the Royal Winter Fair where they faced the keenest Clydesdale competition in the entire country. The filly foal class of 1930 was a big one but when the judging was completed, Julia had placed second and Sylvia third, and horsemen in the East could scarcely believe that these two big foals in prime condition had been mothered by one mare.

Jessica was getting old but the two famous foals, like others she had raised, went on to proclaim the greatness of this prolific and faithful and gentle old mare.

23

Joey

The Toytown Express

How the racing fans loved Joey! It was not that he was big and handsome, because he was actually something of a runt and far from being beautiful. But he had courage and spirit in abundance and these were more than enough to compensate for physical deficiencies. On the track he was not always a winner but always he gave his positive best and tried to win. At the time of his death in 1941, his owner said: "He was only a little fellow but he had the biggest heart of any horse that ever raced."

If a plebiscite had been conducted to determine the most popular personality in Calgary when Joey was at the peak of his racing career, the little black Thoroughbred gelding would have been a strong contender to win. Not only was he winning most of his track contests at that time but he was winning enough

Calgary hearts to ensure a good run for anything to which he might be nominated, even though it had been the office of mayor.

Joey, through his mother, Eileen Hoey, and father, Dr. Joe, had good breeding, but as a foal, he was so unattractive that no horseman was likely to stop for a second look. People who remembered the weedy little fellow wondered how he managed to escape being culled long before he was old enough for the tracks. He might have ended up as a stock horse or even as a carcass of horsemeat going to a fox ranch. When Joey and his mother sold together for the mean sum of $185, it meant that the buyer was willing to pay that much for the mare, even though the foal did not seem to be worth taking home. It was the lowliest possible beginning for a horse destined to greatness.

Joey was foaled in 1930, the property of his breeder, Arthur Layzell, whose horse farm was on the Chestermere Lake side of Calgary. Concluding that he was overstocked, the horseman decided to offer a few mares and foals for sale by auction. With depression being felt across the country, it was not a good time to sell horses but Mr. Layzell hoped the excellent Thoroughbred pedigrees carried by the mares being offered would attract buyers and reasonable prices.

Leonard P. Jacques, of Calgary, fancied a certain mare, Juanita Parks, listed with a filly foal at her side. Prior to attending the auction being held at Victoria Park, he called his brother, C. L. Jacques, by telephone to report his intention of bidding on the mare and foal. The brother's reaction was favorable and he concluded by saying: "If you're going to buy a mare for yourself, you might as well buy two mares and we'll each have one."

Arthur Layzell, an able horseman, must have been deeply discouraged when Leonard Jacques bought Juanita Parks and her foal for $185. In view of the slow bidding on the first animals sold, he gave instructions to withdraw the mare, Eileen Hoey, because buyers, in the mood of that day, would have no interest in buying any female with such a poor foal at her side. Leonard Jacques, it seems, overheard the instructions and having in mind his brother's wish to acquire a mare with good breeding, went to Mr. Layzell, saying that if he would bring Eileen Hoey and her unhandsome foal to the ring, he would start the pair at the same amount he had paid for Juanita Parks. Mr. Layzell agreed and the auctioneer went to work to sell the well-bred mare and her disappointing foal. Good as his word, Leonard Jacques bid $185 and the auctioneer pleaded for some advance on the starting offer. But nobody was sufficiently impressed to raise the bid, and finally, Eileen Hoey and her foal to be known as Joey were declared sold to Mr. Jacques on his first bid.

The Jacques' purchases were taken to their new home but C. L. Jacques was plainly disappointed with what his brother had bought for him. The mare might be a fair investment but the foal looked like a misfit, perhaps not worth raising. The new owner was unhappy about the deal and his brother, Leonard, was unwilling to swap mares and foals, even with $200 added. C. L. Jacques was stuck with the mare and her undersized foal.

As the Thoroughbreds from the 1930 crop were approaching second birthdays, some important decisions had to be made. One of the questions calling for an answer was: "Is this son of Eileen Hoey worth training for the track?" Certainly, such a thin and under-sized colt would never win anything for appearance and if he was to distinguish himself at all, he would have to do it in racing. "Take him along," said the trainer, "Doc" Ronald. "After all, if we leave him at home, somebody will have to look after him. It would be just as easy to take him and we can decide later if he is worth keeping."

C. L. Jacques agreed and Joey was moved to Victoria Park in Calgary for some racing education. For a time he was just an inconspicuous two-year-old and then, unexpectedly, trainer Ronald recognized something special about his performance. He was showing speed and spirit beyond what anybody would have expected and the trainer, after clocking him carefully, inquired if he could buy a half interest in him. This sudden interest on the part of the trainer forced a confession of a conviction, that this "little guy" could be great. "He really wants to be a racehorse."

Joey's first race was at Winnipeg, just as his last western race, eight years later, was at Winnipeg. In the first one, on May 23, 1932, Joey, 14¾ hands high and the smallest horse in the field, attracted practically no attention until he romped home, a winner. Most horsemen passed the success lightly, saying it would not happen again. Joey's trainer did not agree: "This little cuss has something you don't see every day," he was saying.

Trainer Ronald was right and Joey, starting six times in that season, won four races — including the Winnipeg Futurity — and placed second and third in the other two contests, ending as the Best Two-Year-Old of the Year.

Joey grew slightly to measure 15 hands although he was still far from being a model of Thoroughbred type. His charm came from within — drive and fire and determination — and his popularity soared. His racing career seemed to reach a peak in 1935 when he started in eighteen races to win nine of them, place second in four and third in four. The season added $10,630 to his total winnings, a lot of money at that mid-point in the depression. Then, for a couple of years, Joey's racing performance slumped and sports writers were ready to say that the little Calgary horse was finished for the track. After coming last in a Winnipeg race in 1938, Joey was entered in a $700 claiming race and claimed. It marked the end of a long association with the Jacques stable.

Joey was given a rest and when he appeared again, in 1939, carrying the colors of H. A. Bruns, of Montana, he was showing the old spirit which had driven him to fame. Starting thirteen times, he won nine races. And in 1940, his last full racing year, he added enough from purses to make him Canada's biggest money winner during his decade. And it was then, also, that he ran what many people considered to be his greatest race. It was the Western Canada Handicap at Winnipeg, June 22, 1940, and the ten-year-old Joey was racing against a field of much younger horses. As it happened, rains had left the Winnipeg track looking like a mire and were still falling when the horses went to the post. Joey, notwithstanding his age, was the favorite but he started poorly — as he did so often. It seemed to be almost a rule in his racing to be far back in the early part of a performance, making it necessary to work all the harder to win. Halfway through that Winnipeg race, he was appearing like an "also ran." Then, finding his stride, he began a drive through the mud such as spectators could never forget. Covered with mud, his eyes almost cemented closed with gumbo, he bore forward to win by a head and bring racing fans to roar their admiration. It made James Speers remark that not even Man o' War could have brought as much delight to spectators that day.

In the next year, while plans were being made for Joey's retirement from the track, he was taken to Winnipeg by special train to help in promoting the Victory Loan Campaign. As the leading Canadian-bred racing horse of the decade, he was formally welcomed by Mayor John McQueen at the City Hall and then a cheque for an amount equal to half of Joey's lifetime earnings was presented for the purchase of Victory Bonds by James Speers. It was good publicity because Joey was an acknowledged hero.

The little horse with the big racing record — 187 times to the post, 41 times a winner, 40 times in second place, 28 times in third — was taken back to Calgary. Plans were being made for a formal retirement, after which Joey would live quietly on H. A. Bruns' ranch in Montana. But on August 15, 1941, the gallant Joey died. Horsemen were saddened. Charles Yule, Manager of the Exhibition and Stampede, agreed that Joey should be buried right there on the grounds, a hundred yards or so from the track on which the great little horse — "The Toytown Express," as they called him — had obtained his elementary racing education. And to quote a horseman who was present: "There were a lot of sad faces at that funeral."

Men in the racing world would not forget Joey, courageous, tireless and honest.

24

Air Pilot

The Hurricane Jumper

Horsemen who saw the dashing black Standardbred gelding, Air Pilot, taking the jumps at prairie horse shows in the decade prior to 1955 could never forget him. He did not always win but always he stole the show in his own way. In point of courage, he was unsurpassed and no jumper was more spectacular. No show horse of his time could bring spectators to sit on the edge of their seats like Air Pilot. Quite appropriately he might have carried the name Javelin or Rocket.

It was a time of great jumping at prairie horse shows. Any event bringing together such performers as Air Pilot and Garylad from Regina, Bouncing Buster from Brandon, Cool Customer and Gay Lad from Calgary, and Misty Morning and Copper

King from Winnipeg, was bound to be an excellent contest. But regardless of which horse won the trophy, the loudest cheers were likely to be for the two old-timers, the personable Bouncing Buster and the spectacular Air Pilot. They were two grand actors, never suffering from stage fright and never giving a dull performance.

Air Pilot was foaled in 1933, raised on the Russian thistle fare of that period and, in due course, was broken to drive in light harness. But his instinct was to race rather than jog in the conventional manner and not many people at that time of drought and depression could find an interest in racing. Nobody was impressed by the young horse until Dr. N. V. James, of Regina, came that way.

The Regina veterinarian, ever an admirer of good horses, was arrested by this animal's bold nature, his speed, excellent muscling, and refined feet and legs. Sensing something previously unrecognized, Dr. James resolved to buy him. A buyer with seventy-five dollars could still acquire almost any horse in the country at that time, 1941. And so Air Pilot was brought to Regina.

Dr. James understood horses and the black gelding was introduced to a jumping course. He was awkward and often knocked down even the low obstacles. But unusual courage showed clearly from the beginning and regardless of his chance of getting over a jump, he never refused to try. The horse had obvious talent but there was one serious problem; it was in controlling him when on the jumping course. Whether due to nervousness or an urge to test every jump with which he was confronted, the very sight of jumping obstacles made him furiously eager. When headed toward the jumps, he dashed madly at them and either cleared them or crashed through them.

With training, Air Pilot's jumping improved but the wild manner in which he galloped around the course never changed. Horse-show patrons loved to watch this demon jumper, always expecting him to crash or complete his performance by jumping the ringside fence and landing in the bleachers. There was sympathy for the person in the saddle — usually a girl — but, strange as it seemed, Air Pilot's riders escaped with very few injuries, partly because they had no worries about the horse ever refusing and coming to a sudden and hazardous halt in front of a jump. He might crash into an obstacle that was too high for him but, try to escape or refuse, never.

Year after year, Air Pilot went over the prairie horse show circuit. Sometimes he emerged as the champion jumper; sometimes he did not. Always, however, he was a sensation. Always he was the epitome of courage. As he bore madly down upon a high one, it was easy to imagine him saying something to himself: "Maybe I can't get over this one but nobody will ever be able to say I didn't try. Here goes."

His best jump. six feet and four inches, was the highest ever made by a Saskatchewan horse. It was recorded at Calgary.

What Air Pilot spectators saw in the jumping ring seemed dangerously wild, but when returned to his stall, the horse was at once a quiet and gentle animal. With this dual personality and only the wild phase showing when in the ring, he never won public affection like his contemporary, Bouncing Buster. But with his unfailing willingness, his fire and determination and courage, he won something that became quite evident on the occasion of his official retirement in 1955. There were not many dry eyes among the 4,000 people who were present to witness it.

The formalities of retirement took place at the

Calgary Horse Show. As the old black horse circled the ring, the man in the saddle was Barney Willans, who had put him over his best jump. And in the background was a jumping standard with the top bar set at six feet and four inches, the height the horse had cleared in the same ring a few years previously. The top bar was just about three and a half hands higher than the horse himself. When the old fellow saw the jump, he wanted to try it and had to be restrained. He seemed to forget that he was twenty-two years of age and should not be tackling anything so extreme.

While nearly a dozen of Western Canada's top riders who had ridden Air Pilot over competition jumps at one time or another were present, the ringside commentator told that the old horse was making his last public appearance and would live, henceforth, where pasture and hay were abundant and good.

From the electric organ came the strains of Old Faithful. A wreath of fresh flowers was placed about the old campaigner's neck. Four thousand people clapped madly as they would for any other hero and Air Pilot was ridden from the ring for the last time. It was a nice tribute to a great horse and it proved again that good horses can capture places of genuine affection in human hearts.

Dr. James, who discovered the horse's hidden talents and developed them, admitted satisfaction that he and Air Pilot were growing old together and would retire together. In promising that the old horse would have good care and good fodder as long as he lived, Dr. James was very serious. The horseman's choice as a place for retirement was on Vancouver Island. There he found the two prerequisites: a pleasant home for himself and grassy fields for Air Pilot. There Dr. James died in 1959 and there Air Pilot died soon after.

25

Brooms

Character of a Gentleman

Among the nicely wrapped packages delivered at the University of Saskatchewan during the week of Christmas, 1944, was one addressed to: "Mr. Brooms, the nicest horse in the whole world, with love from Linda, nearly eight years old."

The parcel contained a bunch of carrots, a paper bag filled with rolled oats, and an envelope containing salt. Linda's last name was never discovered but she was one of many admirers — young and old — of the Thoroughbred stallion, Brooms, spending the evening of his life on the University farm at Saskatoon. There he occupied the brightest box stall and received the best attention. Quickly he made friends with local horsemen who came to see him. Always they were impressed by his proud character and gentle manner.

As a Thoroughbred, he belonged to the second oldest breed of horses in the world — second only to the Arabian. Developed in England where racing was a popular sport for hundreds of years, Thoroughbreds were taken to many parts of the world to win recognition as the leading racing breed. Kentucky became a North American stronghold and there — where blueblood meant Thoroughbred — a brown colt was born in 1925 and given the name of Brooms. The name was taken from that of the colt's father, the well-known race horse called Broom-stick.

The young animal's fine racing prospects didn't escape attention and, as a yearling, he was sold for $20,000, the highest price paid for a colt in that year. As soon as he was old enough, Brooms was trained for the race track and responded with bursts of speed which made him look like a champion. In his first ten races he won prize money totaling $58,380. His greatest racing success was in winning the Hopeful Stakes in 1927. But the race track is not without danger, and in the very next race, Brooms fell and injured a leg. When it was apparent that the leg would be permanently weakened, Brooms was retired from the track.

Some years passed and then Brooms was bought by James Speers, of Winnipeg, a man gaining reputation as a breeder of superior Thoroughbreds. For his Whittier Park Farm near Winnipeg, Mr. Speers had gathered some of the best mares and stallions of the breed and the success of race horses of his raising gave him the title of All-Canadian Leading Breeder, first in 1939 and many times thereafter. The fame of Brooms grew ever greater. Sons and daughters won some of the biggest races in both the United States and Canada. One was Indian Broom, a horse which on April 11, 1936, ran a mile and one-eighth in one minute, forty-seven and three-fifths seconds, to establish a world record for the distance.

Anyway, late in 1943, when Brooms was eighteen years old, Mr. Speers presented him to the University of Saskatchewan. "The only reservation in the gift," Mr. Speers wrote, "is that when his usefulness is over, he be destroyed humanely." Actually, there was another reservation of a more personal nature to which reference will be made.

Brooms arrived at his new home on November 28, 1943. At that time he weighed 1,285 pounds and stood 15¾ hands high — about average for a Thoroughbred stallion. Considering age, he was active and handsome and gay. Before very long he confirmed Mr. Speers' opinion when he wrote: "I think he has one of the grandest dispositions I have ever encountered in a stallion."

Under the roof of the huge University barn, Brooms felt at home and enjoyed life. He liked the people who came to visit. He was on good terms with the Palomino stallion, Laddie, along with whom he was frequently taken out under saddle. Laddie carried a stock saddle and Brooms a flat saddle. On one occasion things were reversed and the stock saddle was placed on Brooms' noble back. It annoyed him greatly and he sulked; it was not his kind.

Came the autumn of 1946. The member of the staff who had accepted Brooms on behalf of the University was leaving his position, moving to Winnipeg. For a farewell bridle path adventure together, Brooms was saddled and man and horse followed the river trail they had traveled together many times on Saturday and Sunday afternoons. It was one of those glorious fall days when prairie landscape is at its best. Everything seemed ideal for an afternoon out-ing away from city crowds and noises — everything except that Brooms was noticeably lame. It was the leg which had forced his retirement from the race track many years before. The lameness was slight at a walk but bothering the old horse so much at the canter that there would be no fun in it for either horse or rider. Under the circumstances, both were satisfied to remain at the walking gait.

As they sauntered leisurely over the trail near the broad South Saskatchewan, a saddle horse and youthful rider, with an amateur's foolish notions about the need for speed on a pleasure ride, came from behind and passed at a fast gallop. At once Brooms was alert; at once he was conscious of his Thoroughbred breeding; he couldn't let another horse pass him. How could an old race horse restrain the instinctive urge to be off? Forgetting his twenty-one years and lame leg, he was away at a run. Momentarily, he was a young Thoroughbred breaking from the starting post, all excited at the prospect of a race. The rider tightened the reins to hold the old horse in but it was to no avail. This was a race and no Thoroughbred would be stopped in the middle of a test.

In less than a minute, Brooms overtook and passed the other horse and then, apparently satisfied, he slackened his pace, became once again an old horse with a lame leg. It was Brooms' last race and he won it.

As the horseman in question was about to leave the University of Saskatchewan, he recalled the second of two conditions under which the stallion had been presented by Mr. Speers: the horse was to be destroyed in a humane way if and when this man left the institution. The horseman wrote to Mr. Speers, explained his resignation, added that he had reviewed the case of Brooms with other members of the staff. If it were still Mr. Speers' wish, the horse would be destroyed right away.

But there was no reply to the letter. The Saskatchewan man moved to Winnipeg. Then a year and a half later — on the last day of 1947 — he received a telegram from Saskatoon telling that "Brooms died at 9:30 last night." At once a phone call was made to Mr. Speers to report the death of his old friend — death from natural causes. Said Mr. Speers: "Guess I'll not have to answer that letter you wrote over a year ago. I didn't want to say destroy him."

There are still those horsemen who stroll through the University barn at Saskatoon and pause at a certain spot to say: "This was Brooms' stall." One of the old horse's admirers wrote: "When I passed his empty box stall the other day, I missed the glossy brown hide, the delicate wave in his mane, the refined limbs and beautiful form, the swan-like neck, the piercing eyes and friendly nicker which said 'Let's saddle up and go.' "

26

Starlight Koncarness

Forty-nine Times a Champion

Starlight was a black Percheron mare — weighed 2,100 pounds when she won the grand championship honors at the Canadian Royal Winter Fair for the second time. Like the men who sold balloons and candied apples, she was over the western exhibition circuit so often, she was quite at home in almost any city. Somebody estimated her traveling by freight cars at not less than 30,000 miles.

But that well-known show mare with the best of draft horse type didn't always look like a champion, and for Hardy Salter who owned and showed Starlight, her success might have been seen as a reward for honesty.

Starlight's mother, also black, was owned by A. A. Dawes, a farmer at Blackie, Alberta. She was a big-bodied animal with splendid quality in her legs.

Hardy Salter, who came in the first place from Devon, England, and was secretary of the Canadian Percheron Horse Association for a record number of years, visited the Dawes farm in 1940 and saw and admired the mare and her teammate. He admitted he would like to own a pair of colts from these good mares.

"I'll tell you what I'll do," the visitor said to the owner, "you get foals from those two mares and I'll give you a hundred dollars each for them when they're six months old."

Mr. Dawes was interested. Perhaps he was fascinated in meeting a man who would buy foals which were not yet born. More than that, tractors were becoming popular at the time and the demand for heavy horses had fallen so much that horsemen were discouraged. Through the long period of depression in the 30's, farmers found it difficult to sell almost anything and a hundred dollars for a foal at weaning time seemed quite attractive.

"All right," Mr. Dawes replied, "if these mares have foals next spring, they'll be yours right after weaning. It's a deal."

Sure enough, in the spring of 1941, both mares presented their owner with foals — black filly foals. Running with their mothers on the good prairie grass, the babies romped together, kicked their heels high in the air playfully and grew rapidly. Then, at six months or just after the separation from their mothers which meant weaning, Mr. Salter made the payments according to the bargain and took the young Percherons to his stable in Calgary.

At their new home in the city the foals received good care at the hands of Mr. Salter's Scottish stableman who was quick to point out that the young animals were quite different in type. One was fat and round in the body and sleek in the coat. The other, called Starlight, was tall and lean and rather awkward. The stableman, like most people who saw the pair, fancied the fat one and didn't have many admiring words for the other.

That's the way it was through the winter — one of the young horses getting most of the attention. Then in the spring, a farmer in northern Alberta wrote to Mr. Salter saying he'd pay $450 for a good purebred Percheron filly. That was considered an attractive price and in reply, Mr. Salter described his two yearlings and said he would let a buyer take his choice for the price named. A few days later the man in the North wrote again, saying his cheque for the purchase was enclosed and he was choosing the fat yearling with chunky body. As horsemen normally did business, the transaction was now final and complete; there had been a formal offer to sell and then an equally formal acceptance.

Mr. Salter reported to his stableman that the fat yearling was sold and would be shipped to the new owner. But this news was greeted with anger. What annoyed the stableman was the prospect of losing what he regarded as the better of the two young horses. "Why sell the good one and keep the poor one?" he asked. He even threatened to quit his job if the best horses were to be sold while he was left to care for the poorest ones. "Sell the other yearling," he begged, "but not the good one."

"I can't change anything now," Mr. Salter replied. "The deal has been made. I told him he could have his choice and he has chosen this fat filly."

"Ah well," the Scot mumbled, "send the long-legged one. The fellow won't know the difference and we'll still have the good one."

It would have been easy enough to send away the

145

thin filly, which most people had judged to be the poorer one. Salter hesitated a minute, then said emphatically: "No, the man in the North bought the fat one and to send the other would be dishonest." And so, the plump and popular filly was shipped to her new home and the less handsome one with long hair and bony frame remained.

At summer exhibition time, Mr. Salter, as usual, sent a string of horses for the showring competitions. Having nothing else for the yearling class, he included Starlight. As might have been expected, she did not impress the judge and won no prize. But still her owner believed she would develop well and he was right. As she grew older, she began to fill out and become more attractive. As a two-year-old she was again taken to the summer fairs and at Calgary won a second prize. Regina was next and there the well-known horseman, Charlie Rear, picked upon the two-year-old, Starlight, for the grand championship. After the show, as horsemen sat around on bales of hay to review the classes, the judge's choice for championship was the object of a joke because the young mare was still far from beautiful. But Rear made a prophecy: "You fellows can laugh but mark my words; she'll be one of the greatest show mares of her breed some day."

Sure enough, Starlight Koncarness — to use her full name — gained balance and quality and beauty as she matured and won more and more championships — forty-nine of them at major shows and in every instance with her proud owner at the halter. She understood what was expected of her and would stand motionless in the ring with feet placed squarely below her, head up, ears forward — almost like a statue. Sure, her memory was good. As a young horse she was being fitted with shoes and a careless blacksmith allowed a nail to pierce the tender part of her foot. She kicked the shoe off with such force that it embedded itself in a plank wall at the rear and never again would she stand for shoeing. But under other circumstances she was gentle and kind.

She might have been sold for a high figure but her Alberta owner was loathe to part with her. On one occasion he said he would not take $10,000 for her. She was his friend and paid for her board with satisfaction, pleasure and championship ribbons.

27

Burmese

A Horse for a Queen

It did not happen often that Canadian horses got to see a Queen and it happened only once that one of them became the personal property of a reigning Queen. The particular animal which, by gift, came into royal ownership was a black mare, Burmese, carrying the added distinction of having been a Royal Canadian Mounted Police mount and one which had been part of the internationally famous Mounted Police Musical Ride. The jet-black mare, 15½ hands tall and displaying quality inherited from her Thoroughbred father, made a most distinctive gift, also a most appropriate gift.

To make the present even more meaningful, it could be told that the mare was even bred and raised as RCMP property. She was as much a part of

Canada's famous force as the red coats worn by its men and the reputation for "getting its man."

Every nation hopes to impress its international neighbors. It is doubtful if anything in Canadian history contributed more to the image abroad than the periodic performances of the Mounted Police Musical Rides, started long ago and presented irregularly over a period of some eighty years. At certain international events in both the United States and England, the Ride was considered a highlight and Canadians beamed with pride. The Mounties in scarlet jackets, carrying eight-foot lances and mounted on their good black horses, were said to "steal the show" at the World's Fair at Seattle in 1962, just as they did on scores of other occasions outside of Canada. It was heard many times that these men with their equestrian drill were among the best of all ambassadors of good will working for Canada. There was no end to requests for the Ride to be presented at fairs and exhibitions and many people regretted that it was neither economic nor practical to maintain it in a state of readiness continuously.

Even for the intermittent presentation of the Ride, difficulty was experienced in obtaining high-quality horses of the desired type and color. The fact became very clear that if the drill was to be revived from time to time, something would have to be done to ensure a supply of horses meeting the high standards.

The lowly bronco stock of the ranges served well enough in pioneer years when the principal need in police horses was for endurance, but such stock was not good enough when police horses were being used almost entirely for ceremonial and exhibition purposes. The official preference was definitely for black horses standing 15½ hands and showing refinement in feet and legs. The whole country was being scoured to find the horses needed for those occasional Musical Rides. Some more reliable arrangement was needed. In obtaining horses possessing quality and uniformity, there would be obvious advantages in having a breeding farm directed by men of the force. Such a scheme had been discussed for many years but nothing had been done about it.

Ultimately, while a breeding program was under consideration, there was talk of restoring old Fort Walsh in the Cypress Hills of southwestern Saskatchewan. Was it possible to combine restoration and horse raising? The happy decision was to rebuild the old fort established as a police outpost in 1875, and use it as headquarters for a horse ranch dedicated to the production of horse stock for the new police needs.

In remaking the fort, buildings were located to correspond exactly with the originals so that visitors would find it easy to retrace many of the stirring events in the history of that section of the West. The original post had important trail connections with Fort Benton, Fort Macleod and Battleford, over which the faithful police horses carried mounted men and hauled heavy loads. Indians came, now and then, to steal police horses and some familiar figures in history rode in for important conferences. Fort Walsh was the scene in October, 1877, of the famous meeting between Commissioner James Macleod of the North West Mounted Police, General A. H. Terry of the United States army and Sitting Bull, the Sioux war chief. It was just a little more than a year after the Custer Massacre, at which Sitting Bull's warriors cut down General George Custer's 212 men of the 7th Cavalry and then made their way toward the Canadian border. Canadian authorities were anxious to persuade the Chief and his fugitive followers to return to their own side of the border. The Sioux Chief suspected a plot, however, and refused to go for four more years.

Thus, the new horse breeding program started at Fort Walsh was on land with a special importance in Canadian history. It was also land on which some important pioneer horse ranches had flourished.

Selected mares were assembled and black Thoroughbred stallions were imported. Black had become the traditional color for police horses used in the Musical Ride, just as high quality had become a hallmark and requirement.

And so it was there on the Cypress Hills grass that a prairie-raised mare called Minx gave birth to a black filly foal in the spring of 1962. The father of the baby was the English Thoroughbred, Faux Pas, and attendants said the wee thing looked like a coming champion. The filly, which was to be named Burmese, was one of many foals on that good Saskatchewan grass and did not receive any special care. Actually, for summer months while grazing remained good, no special care was needed. It is difficult to improve upon natural conditions furnishing parkland shelter, good grass and clean ground.

When the time came to break Burmese to saddle, her beautiful conformation and amiable disposition made her conspicuous. Here was the paragon of equine friendliness and reliability. She had the temperament to make the perfect companion. She was exactly the kind wanted for the Musical Ride and in the three Rides for which she was nominated, she entered eagerly into the complicated drills and made it appear that she was enjoying them.

It was not surprising, therefore, that Burmese was the mount chosen from all the horses participating in the Musical Ride of 1968 for presentation to Queen Elizabeth II. When presented to Her Majesty at Windsor Castle on April 28, 1969, the mare appeared like a beautiful sculpture. Her black coat glistened in the sunshine while she posed with head held erect and legs placed squarely under her. Did she know that she was being presented to the Queen? One member of the Force who was present at the time, said: "Of course she knew. She was one of the most understanding horses we've ever had in the Ride. She'll be a good ambassador for Canada."

28

Stylish Stella

Sweetheart of the Showring

When the big gray mare, Justamere Stylish Stella, won the grand championship for Percheron females at the Toronto Royal Winter Fair in 1967, it was her ninth time in ten years to gain the high honor. Horsemen at the ringside were high in their praise: "Isn't she grand — fifteen years old and fresh as a daisy. Look at her muscling — the kind wrestlers like to have — and those clean limbs. Such action, bold and yet as true as the movements in a sewing machine."

Stella's last championship at the Royal marked the climax to one of the most notable showring careers in Canadian draft horse history. The fact was that the championships at the Royal Winter Fair represented only a small part of her enormous list of winnings. For eleven consecutive years, she was grand champion Percheron mare at the Canadian National Exhibition, thus making another record not likely to be equaled in any breed. She was known to have gained as many as twenty-eight championships in a single year and she was as much at home in harness competitions as in halter classes. Victor E. Cookson, of Bowmanville, Ontario, her eastern owner, could tell of showing Stella and a gelding as a team at thirty-two fairs in one year and winning first prize thirty-two times. What a show record was Stella's! It was something to bring justifiable pride to both her eastern owner, Mr. Cookson, and her western breeder, Jonathon Fox, of Lloydminster.

Mr. Fox had vivid recollections of the frosty morning in early May, 1952, when Stella was born. He knew his great show mare, Dragona 11, would be having her foal at any time and was watching with all the devotion of a good horseman. Even during the nights he was leaving his bed and visiting the stable at regular intervals, 12 o'clock midnight and 3 o'clock in the early morning. And on one of those early morning calls, there was the dark-gray filly, struggling valiantly to get up on her wobbly legs. The chance of aiding the baby to stand and get the benefit of the first milk was all the reward needed by a horseman who had been breaking his sleeping hours for days.

But there was near tragedy, as is often the case in the lives of young animals. Anxious to keep mother and foal away from possible infection, Mr. Fox gave them the run of a grass paddock and considered it safe to leave them there at night, even though temperatures dropped quite low during the hours of darkness. Overlooked was the hazard presented by a small pool of spring run-off water at the edge of the paddock. On one of those cool nights, the water froze to form a sheet of glare ice. Onto this the inquisitive foal had walked during the night and when Mr. Fox paid his early morning visit, he was shocked at what he saw. Having slipped on the ice, the filly's legs had sprawled sideways, spread-eagle fashion, and she was completely helpless. "I thought we had lost the little lady we had named Stylish Stella," he said. "She was in the most pathetic position. Having given up, she was chilled and her head was stretched out, with the hair on her jaw bones nearly frozen to the ice. However, after pulling her to the edge and helping her to steady herself for a few minutes, she seemed to be no worse for the accident and got to her breakfast almost immediately. Her legs were swollen for a few days but were soon back to normal."

There were other foals around Justamere Farm in that spring but Jonathon Fox found himself gazing most frequently at Stylish Stella. There was something different about her. "It was easy to see indications of a great one," he confessed. But it was a time when the horse business seemed to have no future. Farmers were buying tractors for field work and most people were saying that heavy horses were not worth raising. Many young horses with good breeding and inherited quality were being sent to the abattoirs. There being so little encouragement from users of draft horses, even some of Stella's half-brothers and half-sisters were marketed at meat plants. But Stella's massive body and refined limbs gave her preferment and she escaped the cruel destiny of a slaughterhouse.

Even in disposition, this mare was superior. She made friends with everybody and breaking her to harness turned out to be a surprisingly easy task because she seemed to understand all about the necessity of doing her share of work. She was three years old when harnessed for the first time and hitched with an old reliable work horse. A steady old horse could restrain a wild young thing and help to prevent a display of violence. Instead of kicking and rearing and trying to run away with the sleigh to which she was hitched, she caught the idea quickly and moved away without giving any trouble.

Mr. Fox recalled the third time he hitched Stella. There had been a very bad snowstorm in the Lloydminster area. Roads were blocked and it appeared impossible to get to town even with a tractor. Milk had to be delivered, however, and Stella and her older mate were hitched to a sleigh for the uncertain trip. Huge drifts made it unwise to attempt to follow the roads so Mr. Fox turned the team to drive with his load across the fields. Here, also, the drifts were high and at one point the horses stopped, facing snow which seemed too deep to get through. As Mr. Fox told it, the old anchor horse, with apparent understanding of the difficulty, began to paw away the snow, much as a man might have done with a shovel. "In a few seconds, the little Stella took the cue and started fiercely to paw the snow out of the way, as her mate was doing."

It was a rough trip and the milk was frozen before it was finally delivered but the horseman had warm and lasting memories of his "brave young Percheron and her most intellectual attack upon the big snowbank."

Then came Stella's introduction to the showring and with it a change of ownership. Shown as a three-year-old at the Toronto Royal Winter Fair, she did not win her class although a stallmate, Justamere Star Gem, a year younger, emerged as the junior and reserve grand champion. Before the big show ended, Victor Cookson, of Bowmanville, dropped around, indicating an interest in buying a good young Percheron mare. He was looking inquiringly at Justamere Star Gem, the filly with the first-prize ribbon attached to her halter. But in the course of conversation, he heard Mr. Fox confess his particular faith in his favorite, Stylish Stella, as the mare whose type and personality would ensure a great future, either as a show mare or breeding mare. The Ontario man bought Stella and the wisdom of his choice was soon confirmed.

Not only was Stylish Stella the incomparable champion at the biggest Canadian shows and the individual to win the special gold medal award offered by the Royal Winter Fair in the Centennial Year for the supreme championship in Percherons, but she proved that she could be the mother of champions. The best demonstration was presented when Stella and her daughter, Connie Laet, were hitched to win a heavy draft class at the Royal in 1966. During that and the next two years, Stella's strongest competition for championships came from the daughter and on four occasions in that period, the younger mare succeeded in placing over her distinguished mother.

With passing years, the great mare's color changed in the manner usual to gray horses. The dark-gray coat became light gray and then white, but otherwise, the mare was still the pleasing exemplification of scale and quality; she was still a dignified representative of the old French breed, with beauty of lines, sloping shoulders, short back, powerful muscles, clean limbs and an easy way of moving that near ton of fine horseflesh which was Justamere Stylish Stella.

Without hiding an understandable feeling of affection for his mare, Mr. Cookson said: "She is very docile and can be handled by a small child. Yet she is one of the great performers in the show business. The moment you have her ready for the showring, she comes to life. Of the many times I have shown her, she never failed me once. She is now seventeen years old and white in color but she is as fresh as ever, just waiting to start the show season, one more time."

29

Bobbie

The Mounties' Horse

Bobbie was tall and black and handsome. He seemed like the perfect subject for an amateur photographer. Like a beautiful girl or lovely landscape, he could make men stand and gaze. Even more distinctive than his appearance was his long record of service with the Royal Canadian Mounted Police. When he retired to a second career at the age of twenty-five, he had spent twenty-two of his years with Canada's "Famous Force."

The black gelding, with white restricted to rear pasterns, made many records. Again and again over a period of twenty years he played a prominent part in the Mounted Police Musical Rides, staged at irregular intervals. In each of twelve different years he was on tour with the Ride, making it seem probable that, exclusive of those horses chosen to play before movie and television cameras, Bobbie brought more pleasure to Canadians and others in the Western Hemisphere than any other member of his species, dead or alive.

As a drill horse, Bobbie's performance was nigh faultless. He could take the lead in the most difficult maneuvers, crisscrosses, spins, changes, and charges. It was remarked many times that the green, young horses in the drills were watching Bobbie to see how it should be done.

In serving Canada's Mounted Police — originally the North West Mounted Police and ultimately the Royal Canadian Mounted Police — Bobbie was just one among thousands of faithful brutes deserving praise. Police horses in the frontier period when utility was about the only consideration were the ones which deserved the most sympathy. Col. James Macleod, in reporting for one of the early years, mentioned that 141 horses stationed at Fort Macleod had traveled 295,222 miles on patrol during the twelve months. The long and difficult marches meant exposure to extremes of cold, inadequate shelter, poor feed and agonizing distances between water holes. The hardships could and did shorten horses' lives. It was a tough existence but there was no alternative to a saddle horse for the police officer obliged to travel great distances. In time, however, the ways of the Mounties changed. Mechanization deprived the police horses of their original purposes and left them with little more than training and ceremonial roles. Fortunately, the celebrated Mounted Police Musical Ride was not abandoned.

In the particular years when the Ride was staged, nothing seen at fairs and exhibitions across the country warmed Canadian hearts as much as the sight of thirty-two scarlet-coated Mounties on thirty-two jet-black horses, all disciplined and performing admirably. The Ride was Canadian through and through — like a maple leaf or the game of hockey — and served to remind everybody of the sterling work of the Force for a hundred years.

Something resembling a drill display was staged at Fort Macleod in 1876, just two years after the NWMP made the initial march westward to take up quarters beside the Oldman River. But an order dated December 19, 1884, showed clearer evidence of a Musical Ride at Regina. Again there was a Musical Ride at Regina in 1887 and, in 1904, the year in which the North West Mounted Police became the Royal North West Mounted Police, a Musical Ride troop visited western exhibitions including those at Winnipeg and Brandon. Thereafter, the Ride appeared from time to time, bringing thrills to people in far parts of Canada and even outside the country.

Producing the ride and keeping it on the road required sizable appropriations and there were times when economy demanded discontinuance. Moreover, for a ten-year period in the late 30's and early 40's, the entire force was almost horseless and the Musical Ride was not being produced. Some people speculated that horses were about to disappear and the Ride would never be revived.

There were still some individuals, however, who believed that horses and equitation offered something of high value in training men for police work and soon after World War II, Commissioner S. T. Wood authorized a revival of the Musical Ride. A troop of new recruits began a regular equitation course and late in 1948, practice began for a new Musical Ride. One of the horses chosen for the reinstated Ride was Bobbie, a four-year-old which seemed to be trying to convince everybody that he should be in it. He had been purchased as a three-year-old and with a proud bearing, a high degree of quality as seen in feet and legs and a friendly disposition, he was a favorite from the start.

Late in 1948, the riding troop made a tour of United States cities and arrived back in Canada in time for nightly appearances at the Royal Winter Fair at Toronto. Thereafter, Bobbie was in twelve Musical Rides, which meant that he was in practically all the Rides presented for a period of twenty years. Twice in that time he traveled to England to help present the magnificent drill in which all Canadians were finding increasing pride, once on the occasion of the Coronation in 1953 and again in 1957. Touring England, men and horses won admiration and friends and Bobbie emerged with a special reputation which was not at all according to plans. Spectators seeing him distend his neck and press his mouth parts against the lips of a police officer at every opportunity, called him the ''kissing horse from Canada.'' But circumstances were not entirely as they seemed; a police officer would simply place a lump of sugar between his lips and Bobbie, with a pronounced fondness for sweets, would reach out and try to take the sugar with his own lips. The manipulations had all the appearances of well-planted kisses and spectators loved the act.

Even among men of the Force, Bobbie was popular. Officers, drawing horses for a parade or an exercise, liked to get Bobbie, knowing that he excelled in experience and had no superior in popularity with the public. Humans could crowd around him and children could crawl under him without fear of being injured. An officer could recall seeing a baby carriage with baby in it being pushed from one side to the other by the shortest route, underneath the horse's body, without any mismovement on Bobbie's part

In the rides of 1965 and 1966, Bobbie was ridden by the officer in charge of equitation, Inspector R. C. C. Williamson. It suited both man and horse. And in the next year, 1967, Bobbie was in service in front of the Canadian Pavilion at the World's Fair at Montreal. The assignment was one for a horse combining good appearance and complete reliability and understanding. Throughout a few hours of each day, Bobbie stood like a beautiful statue and was the object of thousands of pictures taken by admiring visitors. No matter how the human masses crowded in upon him, Bobbie kept his poise and was never known to kick or endanger anybody.

One way or another, Bobbie had a most unusual opportunity to know Canadians and Canadians had an equally unusual opportunity to know him. As a veteran of the Musical Ride, performing in various countries, he must have been one of the most-traveled horses of all time.

It might have been expected that a horse coming to the age of twenty-five would be through working. Not Bobbie. Showing only the slightest evidence of his advancing years, he was transferred to another branch of public service, this time to the city of Guelph, Ontario, there to do guard duty and continue to attract admiring friends.

Most of all, this horse, long in the public eye, should have been a reminder of the thousands of police horses which served in less glamorous roles from the time the Force moved westward in 1874, and the great debt of gratitude due to them.

30

Rex Stonewall

Horse of Many Adventures

Some horses, like some people, seem to be born to live dangerously. They encounter all sorts of troubles and if lucky they survive to enjoy relaxed living. So it was with the chestnut American Saddle Horse stallion, Rex Stonewall. Everything, both good and bad, happened to Rex and he became so well known in Calgary that nobody would consider holding a street parade without him. He was in so many parades that he knew the usual routes and objected when there was a change. He won showring honors and was named mascot of a football team. He was in the cold clutches of horse thieves and managed to make his escape. He carried numerous dignitaries, including the mayor of Toronto, and he escaped the cruel fate of being slaughtered and converted to fox feed by the most uncomfortable margin. His was a storybook career, whether he liked it that way or not.

Finally, having survived the numerous hazards, Rex was retired to relative security, to live with all the comforts and luxuries his owner, Archie Currie, of Calgary, could furnish. But even in retirement, the old horse was not forgotten by his friends, some of whom visited him regularly, just as they might pay frequent calls to any distinguished pioneer.

Life for Rex began on the Joe Fulkerth farm at Didsbury, between Calgary and Red Deer, the real American Saddle Horse shrine of Western Canada. It was to this farm that Mr. Fulkerth in 1928 brought four imported mares and a stallion called The Dare, the acknowledged beginning for the breed in the Canadian Midwest. Canadians were slow to show an interest and appreciation but Fulkerth was unwavering in his devotion and continued to import the best breeding stock and raise the best.

There, under the loyal gaze of the breed's Canadian pioneer, Rex Stonewall was foaled in 1937 while the country was still in the awful grip of drought and depression. American Saddle Horses were hard enough to sell at any time but in this period of dire need, a man had to be an extreme optimist to be raising these horses of the glamour breed. But Rex was an attractive colt and was sold to Jerry Puckett, of Calgary. Puckett introduced the stallion to parading and in 1944 sold him to Archie Currie. Rex became more than Currie's saddle horse; he became a companion. With Currie in the saddle, the horse won many showring honors, particularly in parade and glamour classes.

When Calgary's Stampeder football team qualified to meet the eastern champions for the Grey Cup in 1948, a trainload of local citizens planned to accompany. There would be some parading in Toronto and Archie Currie and Rex would have to be there.

As all agreed, there could be no genuine Calgary parade effort without those two personalities.

The horse traveled well, but at Toronto, instead of carrying Currie, Rex found himself carrying the mayor of the city who had not been in a saddle for twenty-five years and was not particularly anxious to try it again. Apparently, the mayor made the mistake of looking admiringly at the noble Rex and before he realized what was happening, he was hoisted into the stock saddle, with no easy way of escape. He seized the saddle horn and when the parade moved off, so did His Worship on Rex, to capture most of the attention over the route extending from the Royal York Hotel to City Hall.

Returning from the East, Rex was almost as much of a hero as the members of the winning Stampeder football team but there was sorrow ahead, and Currie was parted from his beloved horse. It happened this way: Raymond Clifford, a young rancher in the foothills, looked covetously at the horse and asked Currie: "How much will you take for that nag?" Currie laughed and, failing to sense the seriousness in the rancher's question, replied: "About five of your young saddle horses."

To Currie's surprise and horror, Clifford answered quickly: "That's a deal." What was Currie to do? According to the ethics of horsemen, a verbal deal is binding, just as much as a written contract. He could not go back on his word and Rex was led away. Currie tried to forget his mistake and misfortune.

But that was not the end of the trail for this venturesome animal. A couple of years passed and in 1950, following the sale of a foothills ranch, the horses on it were about to be sold. Horse prices were extremely low and these range animals were about to be shipped to a processing plant to be converted to fox feed. The owner of the stock sent a message to Currie, saying: "If you want Rex back at no cost to you, just come and get him." It was a thoughtful gesture on the part of the rancher but the message was not delivered for more than a week and in the meantime, Rex along with 250 range horses was sent to the Red Top Horse Meat plant in Calgary. Rex, to be sure, was on his way into fox feed.

When the message reached Currie, he responded immediately. Of course he wanted to get Rex back but, as he discovered, Rex and the other horses had been delivered at the processing plant several days earlier and it might be too late to make recovery. Frantically he rushed to the plant and began a search for his old friend. He would recognize Rex when he saw him but the stallion was nowhere to be found. It was confirmed that the chestnut horse was one of those delivered from the foothills ranch and had not been slaughtered. What could have happened? The corral fences were too high to be jumped. There was only one explanation: Rex had been stolen from the yards. The police authorities were notified and a district-wide search was started.

Radio announcers were asked to broadcast the stallion's description. Currie would not rest until Rex was located. Five days passed and then came a clue; a mail carrier reported seeing a horse answering the description in a stable at Bowness. The report was that the horse had been found in a private garden and was stabled to minimize the damage. Currie rushed to Bowness, and to his happy surprise, the stray horse was Rex. The evidence was quite convincing; the stallion had been taken from the corral and whisked away to a country hideaway by thieves who knew a good horse when they saw one. But Rex, by some means known only to him, gained his freedom and was on his way back to Calgary when he made the mistake of stopping for lunch in a family garden.

Currie brought his old friend back to the stall he had occupied in other years and there he remained in the Burns and Company barn in east Calgary. There he would share the barn with the big black Clydesdales kept to pull the Burns' wagons. Never again would he face anything more difficult than a street parade and never again would he be exposed to the evil designs of horse thieves. The old horse was sure of a box stall, a dry bed, and all the good feed he needed for as long as he lived.

31

Shadow Hawk

The Versatile Black Morgan

The coal-black stallion, Shadow Hawk, neither started nor ended his career in Canada but the story would have lost much of its appeal if it had not been for his years in Alberta and Saskatchewan. Long after he left the Canadian scene, ranchers on the shortgrass plains were still talking in admiring terms about Gilchrist's black Morgan. They recalled his well-muscled back and rump, his refined limbs and proud bearing. And of course they were most conscious of the quality and stamina which characterized his sons and daughters carrying stock saddles on the range.

The general impression was strikingly similar to that made by Shadow Hawk's distant ancestor, Justin Morgan, the undisputed father of the Morgan breed. The story of that famous horse, bristling with equine romance, began when the foal arrived in 1793. His owner was a schoolteacher near Springfield, Massachusetts, where most people, young and old, loved good horses, especially those which had speed enough to pass all other roadsters pulling buggies and sulkies on the trails. Everybody was interested in racing and just about all other community activities ground to a halt — even church services — for a promising test of racing speed. The young fellows, who never heard about automobiles, had dreams of driving rubber-tired buggies with polished harness and fast horses.

Perhaps the schoolteacher saw some special promise in this black foal; perhaps he did not. Perhaps the little fellow looked like any other wobbly newcomer to the pasture field. His mother was said to be part Thoroughbred but nobody was sure about the colt's father. Anyway, it was not long until the baby was developing his own strong personality and galloping exuberantly across the meadow as though he owned it.

When the stallion was five years old, the teacher moved to Vermont and took the stallion with him. By this time, however, Justin Morgan — for that was now his name — was gaining fame. He was not very big, only a little over 14 hands high and not more than 1,000 pounds in weight, but he was strong for his size, agile and fast. In one respect, he was outstanding: he was versatile. If he had been a man, the neighbors would have called him a "Jack-of-all-trades."

The young horse may have been at his best in light harness and hitched to a buggy. In a road race his stride was enough to take him out in front and he loved to race. But his well-muscled body was good for carrying a saddle and his owner rode him proudly.

174

Nor was that all: when there was heavy work to be done, pulling a wagon, plowing with walking plow, cultivating or anything demanding heavy harness, Justin Morgan could adapt to the draft toil and outlast other horses with which he was hitched. His admirers said he could out-walk, out-trot, out-run and out-pull any horse of his size in Vermont. And in reaching the age of thirty-two years, he even outlived most of them.

His reputation spread. People drove miles to see him and generally concluded their visit by muttering: "He's the kind of horse we need, an all-purpose horse with muscle and quality." There was so much interest in the stallion and so much demand for his offspring that the progeny of Justin Morgan quickly took on the character of a breed.

Canadian horsemen fell very much under the influence of British breeds and the Morgan was slow in gaining popularity north of the boundary. Again, it was the impact of a few outstanding horses which brought the breed to public attention. One of those was C. H. "Chay" Gilchrist's black stallion, Shadow Hawk. Gilchrist, a successful rancher in the prairie country where native grasses were short but nutritious, did not forget the tireless Morgan he had ridden as a young cowboy in Montana and became convinced that horses of that breed offered what he wanted most in a saddle horse. When ranching in southern Alberta, he imported a chestnut Morgan stallion called Maximo. The half-Morgan colts were hardy and handy and the rancher, in 1939, went back to Illinois for a second chestnut Morgan stallion, one called McDenny. Then going to the same state for his third Morgan stallion, he bought the black Shadow Hawk, foaled on May 29, 1947. This colt's father was Flyhawk, a horse of fine reputation.

The black foal with no white markings was soon a
proud and saucy youngster and stylish enough to
make everybody stop and gaze his way. While still a
baby, he became the property of Mr. and Mrs. L. S.
Greenwalt, Springfield, Illinois, and at the age of one
and one-half years he was bought by Mr. Gilchrist,
of Alberta. As the Gilchrist ranch stallion, he was
not shown and was not much in the public eye but
many of those who visited the ranch admitted that he
was the first Morgan they had ever seen and almost
all added: "He's quite a horse! If he's a Morgan, why
don't we have more?"

After a few years, the Gilchrist ranch was sold
and Shadow Hawk was taken to the University of
Alberta farm at Edmonton for breeding purposes.
And from there he was sold to go to Saskatchewan.
For the next few years, he seemed to be lost; in most
horsemen's circles, he was just a memory.

In the meantime, the distinguished stallion,
Flyhawk, died in Illinois and the Greenwalts were
anxious to obtain a replacement of equal quality.
That, they knew, would not be easy. They searched
in various directions, without success, and then recalled the black yearling sold to Gilchrist of Canada
some ten years before. They remembered the young
horse as one with unusual promise and they liked his
pedigree. Their intuition seemed to be telling them
something and they began to wonder if Shadow
Hawk might be the best horse for their purpose. But
after his ten years in Canada, they reasoned, there
would be only a small chance of finding and recover-
ing him. Would he be living? If living, where would
he be? And if he could be found, what chance would
there be of buying him?

Most observers would have said it was folly to
spend time and money in the pursuit, but for these

Illinois horsemen, the hunch was growing stronger that the coal-black Shadow Hawk they had not seen since he was a yearling possessed the superior qualities they were so eager to have in their stallion. They wrote letters, sent telegrams and after a period of patient investigation, their efforts were rewarded by discovery. They located Shadow Hawk on the Frank Yeast ranch at Fox Valley in southwestern Saskatchewan. The investigation continued, and to the Greenwalt joy the aging horse was still "perfectly sound," with "the best of legs and feet." To crown their satisfaction, the Greenwalts were able to buy him and bring him back to his birthplace. Writing affectionately about the recovery, Mrs. Greenwalt said: "Mr. Greenwalt and I drove approximately 3,500 miles with trailer to get him." They were happy and Shadow Hawk seemed to recognize them as old friends and was happy too.

For the next ten years the great black horse was at home at Greenwalt's Highview Farm. Occasionally he was taken to horse shows and although making his first showring appearance at the age of thirteen years, he distinguished himself by winning prizes in classes which would have seemed completely foreign to the ranch stock of which he was a part in both Alberta and Saskatchewan. Nobody would have expected an aging range stallion to be winning prizes in three-gaited classes in the Eastern States or to be winning third prize in the Thousand Dollar Land of Lincoln Saddle Class at the 1961 Illinois State Fair, after only three weeks' preparation under English saddle. It left no doubt about the versatility of the breed in general and the ageless Shadow Hawk in particular.

In 1969, the Greenwalts loaned Shadow Hawk to their friends, Patricia and Donald Long, of New

York State. It was while there that he developed an internal disorder and had to be "put to sleep," on March 1, 1973, age twenty-six. "He leaves us," wrote Mrs. Long, "with only pleasant memories of him, for he was a gentleman in every sense of the word. But he leaves us richer by far for the offspring by him here in the East, produced right up to the very last year of his life."

Strange are the fortunes of men and horses.

32

Chloe King

Natural Fondness for the Showring

A prominent Canadian admitted that every time he saw a passenger train, he had an urge to board and be going. The half-Arabian gray mare, Chloe King, had similar instincts; every time she saw a horse trailer with the ramp down, she wanted to enter and be on her way to the next horse show.

Most horses are "home-bodies" with no particular desire to be gallivanting far from their own barns and pastures. But there were exceptions and Chloe would have to be remembered as one of the "gad-abouts" with an ever-present desire to travel. In her life, travel meant another horse show with fresh opportunities to exchange glances with strange horses and test the feed in other stables. Generally, she was a winner, but whether collecting championships or not, she loved the atmosphere of the horse show,

179

loved the smell of the tanbark, loved the bright lights and the cheers from spectators. The more a crowd applauded, the more brilliantly Chloe stepped.

No doubt her enthusiasm for the show contests accounted in part for the success which made her one of the greatest show hacks of her time. But while most horsemen knew her as a consistent winner with beautiful balance of body, high quality in her limbs and unusual grace in movements, her successive owners remembered her mainly as "the gentle Chloe," one of "the really brilliant horses."

Recalling that Chloe left her with treasured memories, the mare's last owner, Mrs. Betty Ross, of Edmonton, said: "She was splendid company, sometimes amusing, always interesting. She could make you laugh with her antics around the stable, cry when she out-thought you, and fairly burst with pride when she captured yet another ribbon to be added to her collection." When the contest was completed and horse and rider were back at the stable, the mare wanted to be complimented and then she would respond by burying her velvet-soft muzzle in her owner's hands.

She was not above some mischief, perhaps teasing calves running in the same pasture or annoying the other horses. She became an expert at opening gates and untying knots when she wanted more freedom. But notwithstanding her love of travel, she would not stray far away when she gained freedom from a halter or box stall.

The lovable Chloe was from an Arabian father called Radar King, and a Standardbred mother, Kando, and was foaled in Montana in 1949, then purchased as a dapple-gray two-year-old by C. W. Ross, of the P. V. Ranch, Evansburg, Alberta. Asked why he bought her, Cliff Ross replied simply

and honestly: "Why? Because she looks so beautiful."

It was not long until the steel-gray filly, with Gail
Ross — then nine years of age — in the saddle, was
winning showring honors. Chloe and Miss Gail
seemed like a perfect combination and loyalty and
understanding between them grew rapidly. Both
were destined to win horse-show distinction.

Normally, it is presumed that a rider will make
the showring decisions and then communicate the
proper commands to his or her horse. In Chloe's
case, however, this was not always the way. The
brilliant mare seemed to know what should be done
and would not always wait for instructions from the
saddle. Obviously, she could anticipate ring proce-
dure and was often a few seconds early in changing
gaits. A judge on one occasion complained that the
gray mare in the ring appeared to be overhearing his
instructions to the ringmaster and changing obe-
diently even before the ringmaster had time to issue
the official command. "I know that scamp," the
ringmaster replied. "She's just in a hurry to get her
ribbon. She's a clever one."

There was no doubt; the intelligent mare knew
exactly what she was supposed to do in the ring, and
gave the impression at entering of saying to her rider:
"Now, you just sit there and leave everything about
this exercise to me."

At the moment of entering the ring, the mare
knew she was being watched and adopted her most
glamorous appearance, stepping gaily, arching her
neck gracefully, and carrying her Arabian tail with a
proud flourish.

The mare's admiring friends remembered the
time when that beautiful Arabian tail met with
tragedy; calves in the horse pasture chewed nearly

all the long gray hair off, leaving only the ugly stump. It was just before a show and without a tail, Chloe would be an object of ridicule. Something had to be done and a frantic search was made for something which would make good the deficiency. A white tail switch was discovered at Tony Zeigler's stable and by patient effort it was successfully braided into the few strands of hair remaining on Chloe's ugly stump. Chloe disapproved at first but then accepted, and when it was time to enter the ring, she carried the artificial tail with characteristic grace, attracted the judge and spectators as usual, and won the class.

Chloe became one of the best-known horse show personalities in all of Alberta. Discerning horsemen looked for her in the hack classes; youngsters inquired about her and a show manager was known to confess: "Chloe King isn't here yet. We can't start the show until that lady arrives."

Chloe lived to be seventeen years of age, a kindly and lovable creature to the end. At that point, however, she developed a serious ailment and when it was pronounced incurable, her fond owner, wishing to spare the mare from any needless pain, accepted the professional advice to have her "put to sleep." Chloe was obviously sick and failing but when the horse van came to take her away for the last time, the old campaigner supposed it meant another horse show and "perked up" at once, mustering her failing strength to stagger valiantly up the ramp and into the vehicle. Needless to say, among those who knew the Chloe courage and witnessed this display of spirit as she was about to take her last ride, there were no dry eyes.

Everybody loved Chloe King and those who loved her did not forget her.

33

Silver Sport

Slightly Unpredictable

The person who said "The wildest colts make the best horses" might have been thinking of the Palomino gelding, Silver Sport, one of the greatest cutting horses in Canadian history. Lyall Roper, of Edmonton, rode him to the Canadian Cutting Horse championship in 1963 and when, in 1968, at age of twenty-one he rated ninth among Canadian horses, it was the fifth time in six years that he qualified for a place among the "Top Ten."

But Silver Sport was much more than a cutting horse. He was an animal that would live in legend, a fighter, a bucker, a worker, a scamp and a quaint equine character. Anything Sport undertook to do, he did thoroughly, sometimes violently. In the course of his varied careers, he left people bewildered from trying· to analyze the processes in his personality. They could not understand him but they had to chuckle at the strange quirks in a horse which would buck and dump his rider and then stand patiently and charitably by until the bruised fellow picked himself up and remounted. And they had to respect and admire the skill and determination he brought to competitive cutting.

Sport was foaled in New Mexico, in 1947, and his owner saw the baby as a promising stock horse. With good Quarter Horse breeding, he would have the muscle and stamina and instincts for an ideal cowboy's mount. And with a stylish Palomino coat, there would be added reason for an owner's pride. But when the colt turned three years of age and was being broken to bridle and saddle, his true character began to emerge and his owner found reasons for misgivings. There was something strangely different about this one. With golden-colored coat and gay manner, he was a sparkling beauty. But what was this flaw in his disposition?

Breaking him was going to be difficult. That much was increasingly obvious. The colt had a mind of his own. Some of the qualities of an outlaw were showing. Instead of surrendering to a domesticated role and becoming a gentle stock horse, this one rebelled periodically, threw a tantrum and bucked to unseat anybody who happened to be on him. The idea of training him to be an obedient show horse for western saddle classes was abandoned. His conduct was so unpredictable and at times so bad that even the work-a-day cowboys on the New Mexico range wanted to have as little as possible to do with him. In a moment of exasperation, Silver Sport's owner traded him for a pair of second-hand riding boots — not very good ones at that. Thereafter, Sport, like the proverbial bad penny, was changing hands again and again. That nobody wanted to keep him was not flattering in the least, but in the light of his rebellious spirit, it was quite understandable.

And then one of his owners had an idea: if this horse was so determined to buck, perhaps he should be in rodeo where he could kick and disport to his heart's content and maybe win some legitimate distinction in doing it. Sport became a professional bucking horse, traveled the rodeo circuit and generally succeeded in dashing cowboy hopes to the ground.

Parts of the story of Sport's life have become lost but it is presumed that he was an itinerant rodeo horse for a few years and was then withdrawn by somebody who admired his color and fine conformation and sensed some hidden talents. Sport was introduced to cow-cutting and responded with a surprising display of desire and skill. He was still temperamental and would still buck if there was the least provocation, but when he considered the circumstances to be suitable, he entered eagerly into the task of cutting a cow from a herd and, by intent effort and nimble footwork, keeping her separated against her will. He was an immediate success and was attracting the attention of horsemen up and down the state of California when, in 1962, Lyall Roper bought him and brought him to Alberta.

First of all, man and horse had to learn to know each other and that was not easy. "First time I bridled him," his new owner reported, "it took me forty minutes. Nobody could say he was mean but after I was pitched a few times, I realized that many things had to be done his way. In a two-horse trailer, for example, he had to be on the left side or he'd make trouble. He was a left-hand traveler. The day I made a mistake and loaded him on the right side, he almost kicked my trailer apart."

He had lots of idiosyncrasies. He wanted nothing loose and dangling about his hind quarters. Perhaps it was the memory of a rodeo bucking strap that made him react so violently. Lyall Roper recalled the day he planned to ride down a river trail, carrying a camera on the end of a leather strap. It was one of the things Sport refused to tolerate and before the rider had time to get the point of the objection, he had landed in the weeds and his horse was standing benignly by, waiting for reunion.

"To mount him in safety," Mr. Roper explained, "you had to have him facing into a corner. That was the way he wanted it." And anybody who, when mounting, made the mistake of touching the animal's rump with his foot could expect an equine explosion. Like a fussy old human, he had his selected irritations and he could react furiously. And yet, as Lyall Roper reported, when taken to England for a series of cutting horse exhibitions in 1964, "children pulled his tail and crawled under him and he took it all like an amiable gentleman." Funny old fellow, he had his own ideas about nearly everything.

On that exhibition tour of England, Silver Sport was one of the stars in the program but he objected to something on the plane which carried the horses across the Atlantic and became so unruly and such a threat to the aircraft that his attendants thought they might have to shoot him to restore order. Fortunately, it was not necessary and when the Canadian horses performed before members of the Royal Family, the Queen had some special questions about Silver Sport.

In the next year, 1965, the old horse became the property of Mickey Collins, of Edmonton, but it did not require any major change of environment for the horse — not even a change of stable. Sport was surrounded by the same admiring horsemen and he continued to perform brilliantly in cutting contests, leading to the oft-expressed opinion that if he had been introduced to cutting at an earlier age and had had careful training, he could have been a world champion. As it was, he won just about everything a cutting horse could win in Canada — including that Canadian Open Championship in 1963.

One way or another, the aging Palomino was becoming a well-known figure in the horse world. And small wonder. At the Brandon Spring Show in 1967, there was a special evening ceremony to honor the old horse on the occasion of his twentieth birthday. There was a big birthday cake but instead of twenty candles which Silver Sport could not be expected to appreciate, it had twenty good fresh carrots and the big horse-show audience cheered enthusiastically.

But the old horse was not retiring. He was still fast and supple and eager and cutting competitions continued to beckon. He could lend weight to the old adage: "an old horse for a hard trail." When lifetime cutting horse performance scores were compiled in 1968, Silver Sport had one of the best Canadian records.

"He gave me some bad moments," Lyall Roper said, "but I loved that old fellow." And horsemen across the country loved him too.

34

Northern Dancer

The Flying Canadian

Once upon a time — May 2, 1964, to be exact — a through-and-through Canadian Thoroughbred won the Kentucky Derby and did it convincingly by setting the fastest time ever recorded for that famous race. Canadians from coast to coast could scarcely contain their delight.

At once, horsemen wanted to know more about this wonder horse, this three-year-old stallion called Northern Dancer. What they heard was that Dancer stood 15½ hands high and weighed about 950 pounds, not really a big horse. His proud mother was a mare called Natalma, his father, Nearctic, and his grandfather on his mother's side, a horse with a distinguished racing record, Native Dancer. To people who were familiar with Thoroughbred pedigrees, it was apparent that Northern Dancer inherited his great racing ability, just as he inherited his name.

At birth on May 27, 1961, the little fellow with bay coat, blaze of white on his face and three white stockings on his unsteady legs, did not appear particularly impressive to anybody. He was just "one of the colts which might make race horses someday." Even at one year of age when offered for sale, nobody was anxious to buy him at the price named. Although a price of $25,000 may not have seemed like a bargain at the time, it was small, indeed, in relation to the horse's total prize earnings of $490,171 for 1964.

Anyway, when serious training for the races started, the little three-year old out of Natalma began to demonstrate his unusual qualities of speed and stamina and courage. The way he responded was something to warm the heart of his trainer, Horatio Luro.

Came the day of the great Derby race and Northern Dancer was fit and ready but he was not the favorite. Most bettors preferred to place their money on the bigger horse, Hill Rise, to be ridden by Jockey Willie Shoemaker. Northern Dancer's rider was Bill Hartack and both jockey and horse wanted, eagerly, to win.

Getting away well in the big field of three-year-olds, the Canadian horse — bred in Canada and raised in Canada — never at any time faltered. He ran like a champion, bringing surprise and admiration to the 100,000 spectators at Churchill Downs who watched him seize the foremost position in the homestretch and drive to the finish, the winner.

"The Flying Canadian," was the way commentators at the track described Northern Dancer after he completed the one and one-quarter mile course in exactly two minutes, making the first quarter of a mile in 22 2/5 seconds, the first full mile in a minute and 36 seconds and the last quarter of a mile in 24 seconds.

Horsemen could hardly believe what they saw and heard about the stout-hearted little horse from Canada and more honors were showered upon him. In addition to winning more prize money than any Canadian horse before him, Dancer was named the Three-Year-Old of the Year, Horse of the Year and even Athlete of the Year. Incidentally, it was the first time in history that the Thoroughbred Racing Association's Three-Year-Old of the Year award went to a horse owned outside the United States.

Only on one other occasion did a Canadian-owned horse win the Kentucky Derby. The horse was Sir Barton, owned by Commander J. K. L. Ross, of Montreal, but this was not an animal of Canadian breeding. Nevertheless, nothing could deprive Sir Barton of the honor of being the first Canadian horse to win the big Kentucky race and he was also the first horse, regardless of origin, to win the Derby, Preakness and Belmont stakes in one year. After his notable racing successes in 1919, there was public demand for Sir Barton and the matchless Man o' War to be brought together for the "Race of the Century." (See Chapter 10.)

Until Northern Dancer, Canadians were inclined to regard Victoria Park as the greatest Thoroughbred of strictly Canadian making. Here was a horse which won the Queen's Plate, ran third in the Kentucky Derby and second in the Preakness. It was a proud record, with track winnings of $250,000 in two years. But Canadian horsemen continued to dream of a day when a Canadian-bred would lead them all in the great Kentucky classic. They were dreaming of a Northern Dancer.

What might have been an even greater racing career was cut short by misfortune. After winning the Kentucky Derby, the Preakness, the Queen's Plate and some other rich races, Dancer pulled up lame — a bowed tendon — following a workout and his owner, E. P. Taylor, announced retirement to his breeding farm in Ontario.

Although out of racing, the little horse with the mighty spirit was not being lost to the old English breed he represented. More would be heard of Northern Dancer and, considering what he could do for breed improvement across the country, observers in 1966 were estimating his cash value at not less than a million dollars.

Northern Dancer was certainly the legal property of the well-known industrialist, E. P. Taylor, who did much for Thoroughbred breeding in Canada, but to a million Canadians, individually proud of the animal's record, Dancer was "Our Horse." He was Canada's greatest race track performer, demonstrating that his native soil could produce horses of a superior kind and that Canadians could develop and train them to make them champions.

35

Necklace

Bucking Was Her Line

Northern Dancer's specialty was racing; Silver Sport's was in outmaneuvering cattle in cutting competitions, and Barra Lad's was in high jumping. For Necklace, the specialty was bucking and she did it to bring distinction to her Canadian origin.

Her original owners tried to make her into a nice, gentle saddle horse, one that would carry a cowboy on his daily rounds, become the rider's reliable partner in the business of roping and, perhaps, be a safe mount for children. There was nothing wrong with the way Necklace was being trained but she was not what horsemen would call a "natural" in any of those conventional roles. Being an ordinary, reliable saddle horse was really not to her fancy. She was hiding something of her personality. Her special aptitude was in being a rowdy, as she demonstrated a few times when she was supposed to be submissive and proper. Not only did she humiliate some expert riders but she gave herself a bad name.

Having seen her performing in some unscheduled and unwanted events, her owner decided to enter her in a bucking contest where she could be as rough as she chose — the rougher the better — and almost at once this bay mare with white face and the marks of quality in her limbs became the fulfillment of the rodeo promoter's dream. Clearly, bucking was her line and, thereafter, her owners gave her opportunity to buck in the best bucking company. She became a traveler, generally moving in the direction of the biggest North American rodeos.

The mare's explosive qualities were such that spectators were heard to remark: "Another Midnight." Canadians listened with pride, knowing that Necklace was a Canadian-bred horse. It added substance to the claim that a disproportionately big percentage of the world's most famous bucking horses originated on the northern ranges. There was the legendary Midnight, Five Minutes to Midnight, Bassano, Fox and others, all of which gained international recognition for the extreme trouble they gave those cowboys who tried to stay with them in rodeo contests.

Necklace was foaled in the Alberta Foothills, near Cochrane where the famous Cochrane Ranching Company pioneered in 1881. The mare's breeding was Thoroughbred on her sire's side. Her mother's breeding is not recorded, but it can be assumed that Necklace's quality was an inheritance from the old English racing breed. She changed hands a few times and somewhere along the way acquired the brand "H". After becoming the property of Emil Chomistek, of Scandia, Alberta, she was used for a time in general ranch work. In 1964, she made a rodeo appearance in calf-roping contests. But she did not care for calf roping and made her protests by bucking when she should have been attending to competition business. After a few such misbehaviors, her owner decided that if the mare would rather buck than take part in calf roping, he would enter her so that she could buck to her heart's content and demonstrate what she could do. Accordingly, he entered Necklace as a bucker at Stavely in 1965 and she proved to be the "surprise package" of the local rodeo. At that and subsequent rodeos she threw some of the best cowboys in the country and immediately caught the eyes of rodeo fans and judges.

The high-kicking mare did not escape the attention of Harry Vold, who was in the business of furnishing suitable stock for rodeo competitions. He bought her for $300. Now she would have a chance to test her bucking powers in some of the biggest and best rodeo arenas on the continent. Rarely did she fail to triumph.

At first she was being entered in the saddle bronc events but she started to stumble and the Volds decided to keep her for the bareback competitions where she was excelling anyway. Thereafter, her record spoke for itself: world champion bareback bucking horse in 1965, 1966 and 1968. She might have won the same distinction in 1967 but she showed some sign of crippling and was withdrawn and given a year's leave of absence from the rodeo. The summer on grass was exactly what she needed and she returned to the arena to make 1968 a year of double achievement. It was a double achievement because while covering the rodeo circuit and winning championships, she was mothering her foal of that year.

Some people said the burden of the baby would restrict Necklace's rodeo performance and she should be sent back to home pasture for the season. But as the records showed clearly, feeding her foal did nothing to lessen the mare's great performance. While the foal was resting between meals, mother was earning her oats and hay in the arena and doing it with all her former flare. She seemed to be getting better, when a nine-year-old horse might be expected to show some deterioration. At Denver, in January, 1969, she bucked higher and harder than ever and the only rider who managed to stay with her gained the very high score of 85 points. With a foal still only a few months old, she might have been regarded as a brood mare more than a bucker. It was to be expected that other men in the business of furnishing rodeo stock would covet her. They did, and the Volds had the satisfaction of refusing an offer of $10,000 for her.

For fans attending the last day of the Edmonton Rodeo of Champions, March 30, 1969, there was an added attraction. They saw Necklace plunge from the chutes in the bareback riding final and promptly unseat her distinguished cowboy contestant, just as she had done on scores of occasions. Immediately following — before the mare had been removed from the ring — another chute gate opened and out popped the 1968 baby, Shoelace by name, the very image of the mother except for the white markings on two front feet. With head held high, the perky baby galloped to join its mother, kicking high and vigorously while doing it. It seemed that the young one had caught the idea and was promising to be a bucker like its mother. The crowd applauded understandingly.

Horsemen have wondered how bucking stock will be provided for rodeos in the years ahead. The

196

supply of natural buckers from the ranges has dwindled. If the supply failed, there could be no more rodeos. The question was obvious: can bucking horses be produced from selected stock as cutting horses and racing horses and Mexican fighting bulls are the products of selective breeding? Men interested in the answer were determined to watch the beautiful Shoelace.

While waiting for the answer, Necklace, carrying her years well, went on to bolster the theory that there is a bit of extra bucking vigor in horses raised on the Canadian ranges. She was "Necklace, The Toast of Rodeo, 1968."

36

Pinnacle

Special Guest of Honor

It was Pinnacle's special night, May 9, 1972. The proud jumping horse had known many special nights when, as a horse-show contestant, he emerged as a champion in his division. But this was a very special occasion, prearranged, because he was being formally retired from competition and was the Guest of Honor at the Northlands Horse Show in Edmonton Gardens. Everybody was talking about the great horse with both the muscle and the spirit to be a winner and which always gave the impression that he wanted to be a champion.

It did not happen very often that the men, women and children attending such a show were moved to accord a standing ovation to one of their horse heroes, but they did it spontaneously on Pinnacle's big night. And why not? The old horse which had delighted thousands and thousands of show patrons through the years was making his last public appearance, and admiring friends were touched to enthusiasm and tears.

With Gail Ross Amdam — the girl who rode the big chestnut horse to international distinction, in the saddle, Pinnacle entered the ring expecting to see an array of difficult jumping obstacles to challenge him. But the jumps were not there; the ring was clear "What's the matter tonight?" the knowing old horse seemed to be asking as his ears perked forward inquiringly. He was puzzled, but with head held high and tail carried with typical gay flourish, the twenty-three-year-old gelding cantered in a big circle, displaying his characteristic vigor and boldness.

All eyes were on the horse. "What a magnificent old trooper," the commentator intoned. "What a truly great contender he has been in showrings all over this continent and in Europe!" The horse-show visitors cheered and clapped. Pinnacle had heard it all before but generally these words of praise came after a notable performance rather than before. This time he was being cheered before anything happened and Pinnacle was puzzled. Then the pattern changed completely.

Pinnacle's rider drew him gently to a halt at the center of the big ring. She dismounted and stood at the horse's head. Other members of the Cliff Ross family gathered around the old horse they had all grown to love. The lights in the arena were dimmed — all except the spotlight which was beamed at Pinnacle, the Hero of the Moment. There was a pause and, then, from a muffled bugle in the hitching ring came the strains of The Last Post. The saddle was removed and a new and bright horse blanket was placed on the noble equine back. A wreath of roses in the shape of a horseshoe was placed on the old campaigner's neck and admiring horse-show patrons, with tears of affection and sentiment in their eyes, stood and clapped.

"I don't believe there was a dry eye in the house," an Edmonton Gardens official noted. "There were more tears than this arena ever saw before."

Pinnacle was then led away, to retirement and ease. For the rest of his life he would have the best feed and the best care that devoted owners could provide. It proved again how a horse can capture human hearts and how successfully old Pinnacle did it.

Albertans were ready to claim the great jumping horse but Pinnacle was not Alberta-born. He was an immigrant, having been purchased in Ontario in 1957 by Cliff Ross, of Edmonton. It marked the beginning of a long and happy association. Within four years, Pinnacle's rider, Gail Ross, became the first junior and the first Western Canadian to be selected for a place on the Canadian Equestrian Team. Together, horse and rider campaigned on the Eastern Canadian show circuit and then the United States fall circuit, adding constantly to a notable record.

At this point in Miss Ross' career there was a serious traffic accident. She suffered a fractured skull, concussion, and a broken jaw in the crash. It was just a few days before her team was to leave for international competition. Friends wondered if she would ever ride again or be able to ride again. Her condition was serious indeed but she responded well to medical care, and just three weeks after her discharge from hospital, she and Pinnacle were back in contests and winning the 1961 Canadian Jumping Championship at the Royal Winter Fair in Toronto, one of the most coveted achievements in the international horse-show circuit. In recognition of her determination and courage displayed at that time, she was honored at Toronto's Sports Celebrity Dinner and named the "Come-Back-of-the-Year" Athlete of 1961.

For four years, Pinnacle carried Gail Ross from one horse-show triumph to another, ever a source of thrills for show guests and horse lovers. In 1963, he won the New York Grand Prix after a jump-off which was remembered by many horsemen as a classic. Later in the year, the same horse-and-rider combination won the North American open jumping championship and Canadian horsemen from coast to coast were proud of the successes. Then there was a period of training and showing in England and more winnings for the Edmonton horse.

But there was misfortune too. When one more placement was needed in order to qualify for the Olympics at Tokyo, Pinnacle strained a tendon and had to be eliminated from the competition. It was a disappointment and meant temporary retirement from the showring, but the great horse was nursed back to a state of fitness and he and Miss Gail resumed the horse show trail in Western Canada. But "Pinns," as he was called affectionately by members of the Ross family, was getting along in years — old for a horse. In Canada's Centennial Year, when the pioneers were being accorded special attention, it was decided to let the aging Pinnacle relax from the strains and pressures of the show circuit. It would be partial retirement, something to be made more formal and complete five years later.

Pinnacle traveled far and always had the best care and attention possible but unfailingly he was glad to be back in his own box stall in the home stable. There he was on the best of terms with the people and the horses around him and there he could try to exercise some proprietory authority. As the self-proclaimed boss in his home stable, he took liberties and played tricks which no other horse would attempt. That he was one of the greatest jumping horses of his time was well known everywhere; that he was also a very skillful fellow at opening gates and doors was not as well known, but members of the Ross family saw the result of the old scamp's imagination and roguishness again and again.

Of course, he had his own intriguing personality and his attendants and friends came to understand and appreciate it. In the showring he was a serious contestant always, but when work was completed, he was ready for some fun — just like a horseman, and opening doors and gates which were supposed to be closed was one of his pastimes. It could happen in the night or at any time when the old horse decided to enliven an otherwise dull stable atmosphere. Not only would he unlatch or unlock his own stall door but he might decide to open the adjoining box stalls to release his neighbors for the adventure of wandering at will about the premises. And when attendants arrived on the scene to find the stable in a state of complete disorder, it was not unusual to see the real culprit in the act standing quietly in his own stall, trying to appear innocent. On the occasion of a Calgary horse show, it was discovered that all the doors in a certain stable had been opened and all the horse occupants were out and wandering around. Horsemen investigated and could come to only one conclusion, that Pinnacle was the offender.

And, as the lady who knew him best could tell, Pinnacle liked to buck now and then. He would not indulge in such nonsense when in the showring but when he and his rider were on a quiet trail, "He would be just bursting to buck and have some fun." She would tell him to remember his age and restrain himself, or at least wait until they were back home and she gave him the cue. He understood. Then, when near home, she would reach back and scratch him over the rump and "the game was on." It was the message for which he had been waiting and he would kick his heels in the air playfully, like a colt.

Naturally, Gail Ross, who became Gail Ross Amdam, held an undying love for the seven-eighths Thoroughbred which had been a traveling companion through many parts of Canada, the United States and Europe. Of all the horses she had ridden and shown, Pinnacle was the one closest to her heart, the kindest and most personable horse she had known. And with his record and personality, it was not much wonder that he came to be regarded as a member of the family, one to be accorded, ultimately, the care befitting an old-timer in retirement.

37

Kim's Kid

Cinderella Horse of 1971

Everybody loves a success story. Everybody enjoys it when a boy or a girl can overcome the handicaps of poverty or illness or limited education to become a great leader in society, and enjoys it when an unlikely colt from a poor man's stable finds the speed and stamina to beat out the best and most costly horses in the land.

Racing was long known as The Sport Of Kings; in recent times it tended to become The Sport of Rich Men. The high cost of horses from proven racing strains and the high cost of feed and maintenance and training made it so. But there was nothing to prevent a poor man from dreaming and trying to have a winner. On rare occasions dreams came true and an owner of small means with a horse of unrecognized muscle and wind beat all comers. It happened in the forty-second running of the rich Canadian Derby at Northlands in Edmonton when the three-year-old bay gelding, Kim's Kid, flashing three white fetlocks and a shapeless blaze on his face, emerged suddenly as the Wonder Horse of 1971.

It was all so strange. The little man, Ernie Camyre, who was the horse's breeder, owner, stable boy and trainer, was hobbling along on damaged feet; and the jockey, Delbert Rycroft, looked as if he would have been more at ease in a stock saddle on the home farm in the Peace River district than in the winner's circle at the great racing classic of the year.

But there it was; the horse which most bettors ignored on that 14th day of August, was the winner. Kim's Kid, going into the race with odds of 25 to 1 against him, was indeed a "long shot." It meant that nobody gave him much chance of winning. But the element of surprise did not in any way lessen the public enthusiasm and more than 15,000 fans roared their approval. It was one of the great moments in Canadian racing history and enthusiastic horse lovers crowded admiringly around the winner, the beaming rider and the modest owner.

The more the members of the racing set heard about the circumstances, the more they marveled at the victory and the more pleasure they found in Ernie Camyre's success. This Calgary man was a lifetime lover of horses and Kim's Kid was his pride and joy. Even if the horse had finished in last position—as some of the railbirds said he would do, the owner would have had no less affection for him.

Ernie Camyre was born at Moose Jaw, Saskatchewan, in 1911, where his father and grandfather were actively interested in racing. During his lifetime he experienced his full share of misfortunes and reverses. There were occasions when his horse was

206

surer of its oats than Ernie Camyre was of groceries. His more youthful years were given largely to sports, but a short career in football and hockey does not do much to help a man in later years. He was playing football with the Moose Jaw Maroons in 1931 when they met and lost to Woodstock for the Canadian Junior Championship. And he played in high-class hockey company in Moose Jaw, Regina and Lethbridge.

From hockey he turned to a trucking operation and then to horses. Not having much to invest, he was inclined to buy the cheaper Thoroughbreds and was not meeting with much success. As he noted, cheap horses are often expensive enough to ruin an owner. He resolved to sell these mediocre animals and buy no more horses until he could afford the ones with the best pedigrees and maximum promise as racers.

But fate was playing tricks upon the horseman, and just days after selling the last of his original string, he was informed about an abandoned and bone-thin mare, bearing the name Makimba, hidden away in an Exhibition barn at Calgary. The mare's owner had fallen upon hard times and could no longer buy feed. Ernie Camyre felt sorry for the mare and when asked if he would look after her, he replied quickly that he would certainly feed her. Very rapidly he developed a fondness for the animal and then agreed to buy her at the modest price proposed; he gave $20 in cash and a cheque for $180. Oh yes, there was an understanding, too, that if and when the mare won a race, Camyre would give the previous owner an additional $300. But in the light of Makimba's shrunken condition it seemed most unlikely that she would ever race again, let alone win a race. But even if the total sum of $500 were paid, the mare would still rate cheap as

Thoroughbreds were selling and Ernie Camyre realized that he was breaking his vow about buying cheap horses.

First of all, the new owner wanted to build the near-starved mare back to normal weight and he fed her the best hay and bran and boiled barley until she looked like a totally different horse. And sure enough, the mare proved to be a good racer and Camyre was glad enough to pay the previous owner the additional $300 mentioned at the time of purchase. After starting 74 times for her new owner, Makimba had a record of 15 firsts, 12 seconds and 13 thirds.

Camyre was becoming devoted to the mare — and then almost lost her. In fact, he did lose her in a claiming race at Calgary for $1,000 and the party claiming her promptly loaded her for shipment to Winnipeg. Camyre was shocked at what had happened — almost sick about it — but what could he do to recover her? He studied the racing and claiming rules and discovered a violation in the claiming of his mare; because the claimant did not start a horse at the Calgary racing meet, he was not properly eligible to make a claim. The case was presented to the racing stewards who agreed that the mare had been claimed in contravention of the rules. The official verdict was that Makimba had to be surrendered and returned to Camyre in Calgary. It was a happy day for both the mare and horseman when she was back in Ernie Camyre's stable.

For the man who had rescued her from starving, Makimba's performance was far better than anybody could have known, because after being mated with Doolin Point, the mare, in the spring of 1968, presented Camyre with the bay foal which was to be known as Kim's Kid. The baby was a gangling thing

and not very handsome. There may have been misgivings about refusing the offer of a man who had
been willing to pay a high price for Makimba's foal,
months before it was born. But Mr. and Mrs. Camyre watched the foal with growing pride and hope
and believed they saw in it the makings of a champion. When the baby was a week old, Ernie proclaimed to his wife: "There's our Derby winner."

Kim's Kid, to be sure, received the best of care
and ate well, even when his owner was not doing
very well. He was in all respects a "one-man" horse.
His owner broke him to the saddle, trained him and
started him on the track as a two-year-old. Perhaps
the owner couldn't really afford a luxury like a hungry young Thoroughbred giving no return except his
company. There might have been the temptation to
sell, but the Camyres loved him.

An automobile accident in which Mr. Camyre's
first wife lost her life, back in 1953, had left him with
seriously damaged feet, permanently crippled and
handicapped in earning capacity. But nothing would
induce him to sell his beloved colt. He did at times
take part-time work at near-by curling and hockey
rinks, and it helped to ensure that everybody in the
family — including Kim's Kid, received regular
meals.

The Kid was given light racing as a two-year-old
and did not distinguish himself, except in the eyes of
his owner. He was developing bone and muscle,
developing so well, in fact, that before another year
passed he won the Potential Hunter class at
Calgary's International Horse Show. As a three-
year-old the gelding was capturing more race track
attention but nobody said he was outstanding.

Camyre was overjoyed when the colt qualified to
enter the Canadian Derby of 1971. Of course, the

race would bring together the best Canadian
Thoroughbreds of the 1968 foaling year and many
people would wonder by what fluke this unheralded
Kim's Kid got into the high-class company. "It's all
very well to run a country colt in local competitions," the skeptics were saying, "but the Canadian
Derby is a tough race for the best horses in the
country." Sure enough, some of the best were entered, including Chatty Cavalier from a rich man's
stables in Toronto, a colt beaten only once in seven
starts as a two-year-old. That would set the tone and
the Toronto entry, it was feared, could completely
outclass the more humble ones. But whatever the
scoffers were saying, it was not having any effect
upon Ernie Camyre who, with the aid of his trusty
walking cane to assist his twisted feet, saw to it that
The Kid was receiving regular rations, tender care
and the right amount of exercise.

As the great day approached, the owner had to be
sure of a jockey, a good one. With more resources he
might have imported a high-priced rider with a fancy
reputation for bringing in winners but here again he
had to be practical and decided to go with a young
fellow from Sexsmith in the Alberta Peace River
country. This twenty-year-old rider, Delbert Rycroft
was not much better known than Kim's Kid and the
experts said he was awkward and needed experience. But the Alberta boy was eager and he listened
to advice. Ernie Camyre did not let himself think
about the final placing but he was convinced that
both Kim's Kid and Delbert Rycroft would give the
best they possessed.

The horses for the great mile and three-eighths
racing classic paraded for the pleasure of the
thousands of Edmonton spectators; the fans went to
the betting wickets; money being wagered on the

race climbed in total to far above $100,000; the Toronto horse, Chatty Cavalier, was the obvious favorite and went to the race at odds of 7 to 5; Kim's Kid, with long odds, was going almost unnoticed. And then the horses were entering the starting gate; excitement mounted; the commentator gave the word: "They're at the post; they're off." The great race was on and the favorite, living up to reputation, took an early lead and looked as if he was taking command. Hadn't everybody been saying that only two or three of the western horses had even an outside chance against this one? Seven's Best, running second, was the most likely threat. But Rycroft on Kim's Kid was trying to stay close behind this pair and doing well. Another Calgary horse, Helkey, was making a similar attempt and running about abreast of The Kid.

The horses passed the grandstand once, then again. They were soon on the backstretch and the crowd roared more intently. There Rycroft pulled The Kid out enough to pass Helkey and be in a position to show what he could do in a dash for the wire. With only a few hundred yards left, it was now or never, and the will to win became clear. Finding some hidden strength, Kim's Kid bore down on the two front runners and before 30,000 unbelieving eyes, came to the finish three quarters of a length ahead of the second place Toronto horse.

Most of the bettors knew they had backed the wrong horses but that fact did not reduce their admiration for the unexpected winner. They crowded to the fence to see The Kid being led into the winner's circle, see a smiling Rycroft still in the saddle as if he did not wish to relinquish his throne, and see Ernie Camyre and Mrs. Camyre embracing the horse they had nursed, fed, babied, and trained, and grown to regard as a member of the family. The stout-hearted horse had just toppled the racing giants and won $17,499 to help pay for the oats and hay and attention furnished by a devoted horseman with only one horse in his racing stable.

As for that horseman, he could not have been more thrilled if somebody had presented him with the Crown Jewels. "Is The Kid for sale?" he was asked. "Would you take $50,000?" They were foolish questions. Would a man sell a member of his family?

38

Peggy

The Horse Everybody Loved

"Everybody loved old Peggy." So said Hubert Freitag when asked about the founding animals that brought his family's Belgian horses to rank among the best in Canada and on the continent.

He smiled, revealing pleasant memories of the old strawberry roan that was his father's first registered mare. In recent years, he explained, horses owned by he and his brother Eddie on their farms at Alameda had collected numerous championships. Most of the best of those horses could be traced to that mare which was still producing foals close to the time of her death at the age of twenty-three years.

Others who lived in that southwestern part of Saskatchewan had memories too. A lady whose childhood years were spent in the area recalled her first visits to the Rudolph Freitag farm. Her parents might have had more serious reasons for making the

call; they might even have been there to count the
children whose father had boasted of having nine
sons "and every son has a sister." The question was:
Did Rudolph Freitag have eighteen children or ten?
In any case, the little girl's reason for wanting to be
there was the hope of sitting on the old mare's broad
back and relaxing the way a visitor might do on a
park bench.

She also remembered an occasion when she saw
no fewer than five of the Freitag children clinging to
the old mare who accepted the load as if she enjoyed
the trust placed in her.

The story of Freitag successes with Belgian horses
must begin with the arrival in Canada of Rudolph,
his wife, and three small children. It was 1927; they
were coming from the Ukraine to make a home in the
new land. As with all newcomers of that period,
hardships were inescapable. The father's first job
with wages was on a farm west of Estevan. The pay
was slight, of course, but after six or seven years,
these industrious newcomers were moving to Alameda to rent a farm and work for themselves. Renting
led, in 1941, to buying the Alameda land on which
son Eddie farms today, and from which were to come
generations of Belgian horse champions.

Rudolph Freitag was known to be a talented
horseman even before coming to Canada. As early as
he could remember he was dreaming of having a
band of his favorite purebred horses. It began with
that crucial step of making the initial purchase in
1943. Having saved carefully for this purpose, he
visited the farm of Arthur Lombaert in Mariapolis,
Manitoba. There he selected and bought the aging
roan mare. His limited savings would not allow him
to buy a young mare, so Freitag selected the
seventeen-year-old Peggy. She was considered safely

in foal but, because of age, bound to be uncertain for further breeding.

Peggy's breeder was Allan Cole who farmed at Chater, near Brandon; she had both good breeding and excellent conformation. Shown by her breeder in her three-year-old form, she had won the grand championship for Belgian mares at the Canadian Royal Winter Fair at Toronto in 1929.

Having acquired the mare, Freitag gloated upon her, but was not overlooking the risk he was taking in buying a mare of her age for breeding purposes. As an in-foal mare she should give him the foal she was carrying, and on Peggy's record, that foal should be a good one. Beyond that, he could only hope. But things went wrong earlier than anybody anticipated. The trip by truck from Peggy's Manitoba home to Alameda proved to be a hard one. Arrival at her new home was marked by sadness rather than joy because the mare lost her foal almost at once.

There was speculation that this might be the end of Peggy's breeding career. Hopes were fading but Peggy surprised the pessimists and brought thrills to the Freitags by producing a filly foal to be named Cookie when she was nineteen years old. Cookie was quickly followed by another filly—Betty Lou—when she was twenty years old, and still another, Bonnie Lou, when the mare was twenty-one.

Nor was there anything ordinary about these three additions to the Freitag herd. They were good enough to set some new showring standards in western Canada. They were the means of setting their owners upon an exhibition course, showing first at the local Alameda fair, then Estevan, Moose Jaw, Saskatoon, Brandon, and ultimately the Royal Winter Fair. At that point the elder Freitag looked back upon twenty-six consecutive years of exhibiting, apart from one year when he did not enter his Belgians because his son Eddie had accepted the coveted invitation to judge that breed at the international show.

In any case, Peggy's daughters Cookie and Betty Lou, after winning the highest honors across the West in 1948, won the gold medal presented by the king of Belgium for the best two Canadian-bred Belgian mares at the Royal. The next year, with Bonnie Lou as the third mare in the entry, the Freitag trio won the corresponding award for the best three Canadian-breds at the Royal.

But it was in this latter year that the great old mare, already recognized as "the mother of champions," died from a heart attack in her stall. She was twenty-three years old with fifteen offspring registered in the Canadian Belgian Stud Book. In the words of Hubert Freitag: "We laid her to rest at a spot on the west side of a nice poplar bluff, selected for its beauty." Then it was recalled that her progeny were winners in nearly every important showring west of Toronto in the year of her death.

There was a loveable quality about Peggy which promised to linger as long as the memory of showring honors collected by representatives of her family. It was her gentle disposition and friendliness toward humans which seemed to be transmitted to her sons and daughters. She liked human company and enjoyed working for those people who were fond of her. The Freitag children, who had certain chores to perform after school, felt perfectly at ease in hitching Peggy to help them. "As a lad," said Hubert Freitag, "I'd hitch her to the stoneboat and haul the water for the young trees in our shelterbelt. Another of my jobs was to cultivate between the rows of trees and cultivate between the rows in the garden, always with old Peggy hitched to the scuffler.

"Kids were safe with her and she was never known to hurt anyone."

39

An Unnamed Cayuse

Owed a City's Debt

Citizens of Calgary, when talking about great horses in their city's history, are sure to mention Barra Lad, whose jumping performance brought a world record. They'll tell about the little thoroughbred Joey, whose unfailing spirits made him a great racing success and a "favorite son." There'll be something about the many-times winner, the Clydesdale stallion Balgreggan Hero, that was judged a supreme champion over all breeds in 1902. And there will be reference to the famous Hackney stallion Robin Adair, that collected his most prestigious awards at Madison Square Gardens in New York.

Of course there were more, and if the horseman is well informed about past glories, he might also recall the case of a lowly broncho of unknown antecedents and without even as much as a name. Nevertheless the creature won at least fleeting fame from a bucking act that unseated and immobilized a high-ranking civil servant from Ottawa in 1884. The performance proved to be of more importance than anybody could have recognized at the time.

A horse failing to rate a better name than "Anonymous" is a poor candidate for immortality, and not even sure of being remembered at all. But every horse deserves a name it can call its own and it may not be too late to confer one upon the Fish Creek cayuse. There is reason to believe that the equine in question was a gelding. And he was, in a practical way, the means of Calgary acquiring the priceless community asset often referred to as Victoria Park. Hence, the cayuse might well be honored with the name of Victor.

The story must begin with the organization in August, 1884, of the Calgary Agricultural Society, the progenitor of today's proud exhibition and stampede. Officers and directors considered holding a fall fair in that first year but decided, instead, to send an exhibit of grains and vegetables to the Toronto exhibition. Later, they would make plans for a local fair when, hopefully, the directors would have an acceptable fair ground.

Then it happened. A. M. Burgess, deputy minister of the interior, Ottawa, came that way to make an inspection of federal lands in the Fish Creek area, south of Calgary. The Ottawa man borrowed or rented a horse and saddle and set out, unaccompanied, to study the various parcels of crown land and enjoy the bright foothills and mountain scenes.

A good horse knows when to buck and when to be gentle and decent. Victor, for the performance of his tantrum, chose a moment when the Ottawa man was daydreaming in the saddle in a spot well back from the trail and beyond the range of human eyes.

Nobody would ever know what triggered the wild outburst of bucking, but cause no longer mattered. The fact was that when the western horse leaped skyward, the federal civil servant was pitched high into the air and landed on hard ground with a bone-crunching jolt. The horse, free of his encumbrance, took off at a gallop, like a schoolboy dashing toward the swimming hole for a quick recess dip. He left the government man aching with a fractured collarbone and badly bruised eastern pride.

Then, as if the hand of fate insisted upon taking a leading role, Major James Walker, with enthusiasm for an annual fair and a hope for a proper site at which to hold it, came that way, driving a team of horses and a wagon. Mercifully, he rescued the dejected deputy minister and, like the good Samaritan of old, took him to where he would have the best care, which happened to be the Walker home.

Nobody would suspect the former Mounted Police officer James Walker of taking advantage of an injured man's helplessness while he recuperated in the Walker house—and nobody said he wouldn't do it for a good cause. In any case, when Burgess was feeling better and still very conscious of his debt to his rescuer and host, Walker introduced the question of the agricultural society and its needs for a piece of land for permanent use as a fair ground.

"There," said Walker, pointing in the direction of the Elbow River, "is a parcel of land over which you have jurisdiction. It would serve us fine, about a hundred acres. Do you think you could arrange something?"

The deputy minister, still in a poor position to resist or argue with his host, made a notation and said he would look into the matter as soon as he returned to Ottawa.

Burgess, as good as his word, studied Walker's request and then wrote to him, thanking him for the timely rescue and the generous hospitality during his days of convalescence. And, yes, Burgess agreed that the piece of land beside the Elbow could and would be made available to the Calgary Agricultural Society at a modest price. And modest indeed was the price proposed—$2.50 per acre for the ninety-four acres. The youthful agricultural society did not have much money, but to acquire this property it did not need much. The land that was to become Victoria Park—or the Calgary Exhibition and Stampede Park—at the heart of the city was purchased for a total of $235.

Nobody doubted that the broncho responsible for the deputy minister's fracture and the detention which brought him under the spell of the friendly Major James Walker, deserved a share of the credit for what must have been the best real estate bargain in the city's history.

Members of the agricultural society and the entire area were indeed fortunate. And the *Calgary Herald*, on July 9, 1884, editorialized somewhat facetiously that the cayuse responsible for dumping the deputy minister deserved to have been nominated to run in the recent election for the Calgary seat on the council of the Northwest Territories. The editor explained that the *Herald* did not take sides in the election contest between Messrs. Geddes and Oswald, and then expressed regret that "no one thought of nominating a third candidate who has probably done as much for the country as any man in it. We refer to the cayuse to whose prompt and energetic action lately on the banks of Fish Creek we owe it that the deputy minister of the interior has thought fit to prolong his stay among us."

In extolling the action of the cayuse, the editor was thinking of more than the needs of the agricultural society. He was looking for clarification of federal land policies where settlers were concerned. And so the editor continued:

"The lengthened stay of the deputy in this part of the country at the present time when lease holders, squatters, and miners are alike anxious to have their various systems of tenure brought prominently before the notice of the Ottawa government, cannot but be fruitful of good . . .

"We think, accordingly, that the Fish Creek cayuse chose his opportunity and his man with a wise and statesmanlike instinct that reflects the highest credit. . . . He is worth six Northwest [Territories] councillors to us, not only for what he has done in the past but for what he may do in the future."

The editor's idea, it seemed, was that the Fish Creek cayuse, after displaying superior judgment "worth six Northwest [Territories] councillors," should now be installed as a one-horse commission or brain trust to work full time for the region.

40

Old Nahanni

Visibly battered and bruised, an old bay mare that appeared uninvited, unwanted, and unheralded in the Foran pasture at Priddis one day late in 1979, looked like the proverbial walking skeleton. Her ribs protruded like the ridges of a pioneer's washboard; her feet were overgrown, suggesting that they had never been trimmed, and her ears were shortened to different lengths as though chewed off by a hungry animal.

Nahanni—as she was to become known—was no beauty, and her disposition was something to match her wild appearance. Even the well-fed horses grazing regularly and peacefully in the field treated her with disdain.

But from where did this dejected-looking specimen come? How did she get inside the barbed wire fence that held the well-fed and contented Foran horses? Gradually the circumstances became known and they were not pleasant.

If Nahanni feared and hated the very sight of humans, it wasn't surprising. The welts on her rump gave indication of blows from a cane or club, and the festering sores occurring in regular rows of three were doubtlessly from a three-tine hayfork. It all told of brutal treatment in the course of capturing and loading the wild horses of which Nahanni was one.

Some questions about the old mare would never be answered, but there should be an explanation for her presence in these parts and especially her entry into the fenced field. Nahanni was almost certainly of the mustang strain and part of a small band captured back in a secluded mountain valley by men who hoped to rough-break the wild things and sell them to make a quick profit. While some members of the captured herd accepted partial domestication without a great fight, others, like Nahanni, refused to surrender their fierce independence and were called outlaws. Partly because of her fighting nature and partly because her ugly appearance left her unattractive to horsemen, the old mare managed to escape the indignities of saddle and harness. Eventually, she was marked for a cut of low-grade horses to be delivered dead or alive at a Calgary slaughterhouse where horsemeat was processed for the fox meat and dog feed trade.

Even in her advanced years, the mare was fast and agile and difficult to corral. She was still more difficult to coax or force up a loading ramp and into a truck. It was in the latter operation, no doubt, that she was beaten with a whip or club and prodded with a pitchfork. Once loaded, however, she and others intended for slaughter were moved to a holding field close to the Foran farm.

Now, as if she was getting warnings from an all-wise and all-merciful deity, the old mare broke away from the holding field. She then apparently jumped a barbed wire fence to join the small band of care-free horses on one of the few farms where an unattractive old horse might have a chance of a compassionate reception. Shortly afterwards, she followed her new companions to the stable yard where the daily treats of oats and carrots were being dispensed. The regular boarders rushed forward to get their treats; Nahanni halted a safe distance away when she saw a human figure. She wanted nothing more to do with them. The other horses could have the oats and carrots; she would keep her distance.

A few days later, the mare's legal owner came looking for his lost horse and readily identified her in the Foran pasture. He made a routine call at the farm home and, expecting no resistance, announced his intention to rope or shoot the wild one and remove what was his rightful property to the meat plant.

The lady of the house had some questions. When she was informed that the mare was on her way to the slaughterhouse, she announced that she was not about to surrender the animal that had come to her for protection and shelter. There was an argument. In the end, the lady bought the old mare, paying a little more than her carcass would have brought at the plant.

Nahanni seemed to get the message that she had been rescued from certain death, and slowly she ventured closer to the person who regularly doled out oats and carrots. Although surprised that nobody had raised a club or pointed a pitchfork at her, she made bold to advance with the other horses until, following their example, she took a mouthful of oats. It was probably the first time in her long life that she had tasted grain, and it was so good that she was ready to run the risk of taking another mouthful, this time a bigger one.

Nahanni was puzzled. The new humans were different and the other horses were showing no fear of them. She became a little bolder. Then winter set in and the horses were given hay as well as oats in the stable yard. The old mare's fears continued to evaporate and one day before Christmas, the lady who rationed the hay was allowed to touch her. Nahanni flinched but the contact didn't hurt; another day she allowed her coat to be brushed and it felt wonderful. Then when she was engaged with her oats, a halter was placed gently on her head and buckled. It was, again, a first in her life, and before long she was allowing herself to follow when led by the halter. The next experience was really frightening; somebody was trimming her overgrown hooves and she was surprised to find that it didn't hurt. Once that was done, Nahanni found that she could walk and run more easily and she liked it. It was as if she had been transferred to a totally new world where humans were not constantly chasing or hurting horses.

All the while, old Nahanni was nursing a secret which she had managed to keep from the good people who fed and brushed her. It may be that she was dreaming of repaying her kind friends. In any case, soon after the evening bale of hay was brought out on a late winter evening, Nahanni disappeared. As darkness settled, the mare had not returned and the Forans were puzzled. But it was too dark to make a search.

The snow was deep and the night was cold, as nights can be at the end of February. But early on the following morning, a search for Nahanni was started.

At the moment the sun was emerging above the horizon, the searchers spotted the mare in the shelter of some trees. She raised her head and pranced nervously, walking around the dark object partly hidden in the frosty snow. Then, as if reassured by recognizing a familiar human, the one who fed and brushed her, she nickered quietly as if saying: "Come and see what I have to show you."

There it was, Nahanni's baby, a bay filly foal with a white stripe on its face and two white feet, obviously nearly frozen. Nahanni's nervousness disappeared and the delighted searchers helped the baby to stand on its shaky legs and get its first drink of mother's milk. The swig proved to be great stuff and the result was instantaneous and miraculous. Then Nahanni, with the chilled and wobbly foal at her side, allowed herself to be led back to the stable yard where there was a dry bed on which the foal could lie in the sun.

The household excitement was intense. It was difficult to know who was the most affected—the mare or members of the farm family. Children, parents, and grandparents came to admire and marvel, proving that few things could be more effective than a foal in bridging the "age gap." Bringing members of the family, their friends, and relations instantly to a common level, old Nahanni's foal did it with finesse.

It is difficult to pinpoint what was so unusual about this case. Certainly, there had been lots of foals born in the snow ahead of this one, whom the family had named Coco. One element was the story-book character of the foal's background—the poor old mother's struggles to escape the slaughterhouse and the fact that by all the rules, the baby should have perished in the snow. Maybe it was the idea that a thin old mare with ears looking as if they had been chewed off by coyotes and possessing neither beauty nor utility could produce a foal that from a few days of age was captivating and proud. It was as though she was boasting of how her mother, in her earlier years had been a hardy mustang breathing the freedom of her mountain valley, and her daddy had been a handsome Arabian with a pedigree reaching back a thousand years.

The alteration in the half-frozen foal was no more spectacular than the continuing change in the old mother. Until so recently she had never had a halter on her head, nor a saddle on her back. She had not experienced a gesture of affection from a human, and had never had a roof over her tough body. Most surprising of all was the fact that she eventually allowed herself to be placed within the confines of that thing humans called a stable.

But as Nahanni's baby grew to maturity with the quality and form of a champion, the old mare was changing her ways. She became the first horse to respond when called, the first to coax for oats, the first to invite a brushing, the first to leave her grazing and come to greet a person she recognized. She, more than any of the horses on the farm, enjoyed human attention and tried to return as much as she received.

Old Nahanni paid her debt to the lady who rescued her. She remained to discharge another and more special responsibility—that of demonstrating for the benefit of horses and humans alike that kindness is the most effective of all ingredients in overcoming even the fiercest of prejudices.

41

Star

A Lifesaver

George Spence, who homesteaded beside the border separating Saskatchewan and Montana, had a lifelong love for good horses and a matching admiration for those little-understood instincts and skills inherent in the equine race.

As horsemen should know, their animals are often the first to recognize danger and among the most successful of all domesticated mammals in escaping the misfortune of becoming lost. Indeed, this characteristic has frequently been the means of sparing humans from painful exposures and death.

And that was not all that George Spence wanted to tell about horses he had known. He would castigate humans for being slow to recognize the horse's emotional traits that caused experiences of real joy, loneliness, depression, sorrow, and even, on occasions, the shedding of tears.

Memorable, for example, was the Medicine Hat funeral for rancher Barney Simpson from Sage Creek. Barney's favorite mare, carrying an empty saddle with Barney's riding boots in a reversed position in the stirrups, occupied a place of honor in the procession to the grave.

That little bay mare was beautiful; in fact, Beauty was her name. She spent her whole life working for Barney, and between the two there grew a strong attachment, loyalty, and trust. George Spence was sure the mare knew what was wrong that day. "It was an engaging and impressive spectacle that met the eye," he said. "The little mare seemed to sense that something strange and terrible had befallen her master. Unmistakably there was a distinct and plaintive note in her call as she whinnied again and again for the return of that master.

"There be those who will say that such things cannot be. Others with a more intimate knowledge of the strong bond of attachment which can exist between a horse and its master, and who better understand the mysterious innate processes that govern the responses of a horse to human care and human kindness will say, confidently, that such things can happen, that the little cowpony knew, in a way not given to mortals to understand, that never again would she taste lumps of sugar from the hand of her kindly master, lumps of sugar which Barney always carried in his pocket to feed her at the end of a hard day of riding." Hence the big tears of sorrow that allegedly trickled down Beauty's face that day.

George Spence sat as a member of the House of Commons in Ottawa. He had also occupied cabinet portfolios in the Saskatchewan government. He served as the first director of the Prairie Farm Rehabilitation Act and sat as a distinguished member of the International Joint Commission. At home, he had his own saddle pony—Star by name—that revealed more of those "mysterious innate processes." The pony was a dark bay with a big star on its forehead. The dark color made him difficult to detect at night, but comparatively easy to see in a snowstorm. More important, Star knew as much about handling cattle as the best cowboy on the ranch; neighbors called him the "assistant manager."

One of Star's memorable tests occurred on a day in midwinter, following a spell of mild weather that caused the Spence cattle to drift far into the hills in the Frenchman River country. Some wandered south across the border into Montana. The morning dawned bright and clear with just a gentle wind bearing a chinook quality. There was, however, a light blanket of new snow, enough to produce serious drifting if the wind became stronger.

By early afternoon, the sky was overcast and there were signs of a change in the weather. "We may be in for a storm," George Spence reasoned, wishing his cattle that had turned southward in their search for grazing were back on their own feedground. Turning to one of the newer ranch hands, Spence instructed: "Slim, throw the saddle on Star and ride down the Blue coulee into Montana; you'll see our cattle and you can turn them back toward home."

Mrs. Spence offered a mild criticism, saying it might be dangerous for a young cowboy who had limited experience with cattle and horses. "It would be terrible to have a frozen cowboy on our hands," she muttered. George agreed that the weather might turn rough, but he chose to believe that the threatening storm would blow over.

The wind grew stronger and by sundown the range was wrapped in a blizzard. George Spence admitted that he was worried for Slim's safety. "It's the worst night we've seen here in years. I guess it was a mistake to send Slim out with those clouds looking so angry."

Huddled around the stove in the bunkhouse, the other cowboys were uneasy, thinking about poor Slim and wondering how soon the ferocious wind would turn their shelter upside down. It was past the usual bedtime hour for the Spences and their hands, but nobody was retiring. All thoughts were with Slim; every passing moment seemed to increase the chance that he was already a frozen corpse. George Spence hung a lighted kerosene lantern outside the bunkhouse door in the hope that it would serve as a beacon for anybody in distress. But it was to no avail because the wind blew it out about as fast as Spence could relight it.

Everybody had that feeling of utter helplessness. How insignificant are man's best efforts in trying to counter the fury of a wild prairie gale loaded with stinging snow and Arctic frost. The cold was becoming too much for the bunkhouse stove and the cowboys were beginning to shiver. Spirits were falling when, without any warning, the door crashed open and what looked more like a snowman than a cowboy stumbled in. For a moment, the man's identity might have been in doubt, but sure enough, it was Slim, numb from cold and frostbitten about the ears, nose, and feet.

But Slim was alive and said he would be all right now. Spence and his men went to work to pry the cowboy out of his ice-encrusted clothes while Mrs. Spence was preparing a hot midnight meal. Slim was soon ready to talk about his awful adventure.

He located the Spence cattle and started them against the oncoming blizzard toward home. But when they came to a wooded coulee, they chose to stop in the most sheltered part and Slim decided to leave them there and come on alone. He tried to keep his horse on what he considered to be the proper course, but before long he realized that he was lost, probably pulling his horse away from the proper direction.

"What now?" Slim asked himself. Wisely, he remained in the saddle. But that was not enough. He remembered hearing about horses finding their way home in the dark and in storms, but he had never believed the stories. Now, unable to think of anything better, he knotted the reins, hung them over the saddle horn, and gave Star his head, saying: "There you are, Star. I'm licked. See what you can do."

Slim could tell that Star changed direction and plodded on, not very fast. He was worried, still less than convinced that the horse knew any more about the problem than he did. He hoped to recognize a familiar landmark through the snow, but saw none. He was growing steadily more despondent, until Star stopped abruptly with his face almost in contact with the stable door, his own stable door.

Although nearly perished, Slim, with a new and finer respect for the blessing of a good horse, escorted Star to his stall and made sure a generous supply of hay was in place in the manger before he staggered on to the bunkhouse to attend to his own needs. There he proclaimed Star as his lifesaver and hero for evermore.

After relating the episode, George Spence wrote: "No contraption of oil and rusty metal can ever come between the cowboy and his horse. You can't speak soothingly to a gas wagon."

42

Dandy

The Half-Pint Horse Hero

He was just a little fellow, but Dandy proved that small size in a horse is no barrier to quality, speed, and equine personality. Guy Weadick said of him: "He was about as big as a minute but he could travel like 'greased lightning' and he had a heart as big as a barn."

Weadick, whose name is forever linked with the birth of the Calgary Stampede, had as many horse heroes as a sailor has girlfriends, but he saved most of his extravagant terms for Dandy, his wife's special saddle horse for fancy roping contests. To him, Dandy was always "the biggest little horse that ever grunted under a cinch."

For years prior to his retirement, Dandy carried Florence La Due—as Mrs. Weadick was known—and her world championship honors for fancy roping in the women's division. With a small lady on his back, Dandy did not seem conspicuously small, but he had to stretch a bit or ease forward on his "tiptoes" to register a height of 13½ hands; his weight was a mere 630 pounds. With such proportions, he was sometimes called "the runt," but not many horsemen would have had the courage to use unflattering terms in the presence of either Guy Weadick or his wife.

Strange and devious were the circumstances that brought the Weadicks and the small grey gelding together.

Guy Weadick, born in New York State in 1885, ran away from home in his boyhood and headed for Montana which was seen as a state-sized school for cowboys. There he learned to ride, rope, and talk the cowboy lingo. He was tall and lean and when seated in a stock saddle, he looked like the perfect occupant. But the fact was that this young man was being drawn instinctively to both rodeo skills and vaudeville. On the stage, he appeared as a natural, a one-man show, rather like Will Rogers, his friend of later years.

Weadick's introduction to western Canada came in 1905 when he and the Negro performer Will Pickett were travelling together. Pickett was an expert at bulldogging; Weadick was his manager. At the end of the tour the two cowboys went to Winnipeg hoping for new bookings, but had the misfortune of losing their horses, saddles, and riding gear to thieves. The Manitoba police had no success in tracing the rustlers, but when the two cowboys obtained a clue, they followed a cold trail to Emerson and then into Minnesota. Extending their search to Chicago, they discovered that the Miller Brothers Wild West Show was playing there and they stopped to see it. Here Weadick's attention was captured by the young lady,

Florence La Due, who was distinguishing herself as a fancy roper and, indeed, as a very fancy cowgirl personality. Temporarily, Weadick forgot about the stolen horses and before long, Guy and Florence were being married and planning a joint career in western-style vaudeville.

In each of two seasons they were in Calgary, riding with Miller Brothers Wild West Show. Then, in 1912, they were back for the city's first big stampede, with the responsibility for planning and management resting squarely upon Guy's shoulders. While he was directing the historic event, Florence was among the contestants and came away with the top prize in fancy roping for women, an award that was symbolic of the world championship. During that same week, Florence bought a new horse for her act, a twelve-year-old raised in the Cochrane district and known as Prince.

At about this time, Mexico was being drawn into rebellion and civil war and the little grey gelding to become known as Dandy was one of the many horses being inducted into the Mexican cavalry. As it happened, one of the rebel leaders, Poncho Villa, with a strong following, managed to cut off a big force of loyal Mexican cavalrymen and pinned it against the south side of the Rio Grande River.

The besieged federal force was trapped with only two possible courses, both bitter for loyal troops; they could either surrender to the rebels or swim men and horses to the Texas side where seizure could be expected. Those in command chose the latter and were promptly relieved of their horses.

By a United States government order, the well-trained and hardy Mexican horses were sold, and according to Guy Weadick, 600 head, including Dandy, were bought by Miller Brothers. A few of

these, again including Dandy, were selected for the
Wild West Show programs.

In 1915, the Miller show troupe, including the
Weadicks, was playing at New York. There they saw
Dandy for the first time. They admired him and
wanted to own him, but Dandy had a special role in
the show and was not for sale.

After the weeks at New York, the Weadicks
accompanied half of the Miller troupe to England.
The other half, with Dandy in it, moved out for a
North American tour. When the Weadicks returned
from England, they set about to create their own
small road show and needed a small horse with speed
and bullet-like starting ability, one that would be a
good target for Florence La Due's unerring lariat.
They needed Dandy and admitted it. But Dandy had
been sold by the Millers and was in private hands,
somewhere in the United States. With determination,
the Weadicks traced him and bought him. Thereafter
Dandy and Florence seemed to belong to each other
and were never parted until separated by death.

In 1919 Guy Weadick was back in Calgary to
manage the big Victory Stampede. Florence and
Dandy were with him. For the little grey, along in
years, it marked his last public appearance before
retirement. But there wasn't much evidence of tiring
or aging in the final performance, of which Guy
Weadick delighted to tell. It was one of the concluding acts of the stampede. As Guy told it, a horseman
looking at Dandy expressed surprise that Weadick
would continue to freight a little grey "not much
bigger than a dog" around the country. "What good
would he be in a contest?"

One of those who heard the scornful remark was
Johnny Mullins, a good roper and friend of the
Weadicks. "Say," said Mullins, addressing the cynic,

"you don't know what you're talking about. What would you say if I told you that little guy is one of the best roping horses on the grounds? Would you bet a hundred dollars that I was wrong?"

"I'll bet you a hundred you can't prove what you've said about him."

"All right, here's my money," said Mullins. "We'll turn out one of those big Mexican steers and give him the usual head start. I'll take Dandy and I'll show you something about fast work. We'll let the official timekeepers decide if Dandy isn't one of the best roping horses of the week."

It was agreed that Mullins and Dandy would win or lose in the regular stampede competition for roping and tying. With Mullins in the saddle, Dandy did, indeed, look somewhat like a big dog, but he seemed to understand the point of it and pranced excitedly as horse and rider waited for the signal to start.

The twelve-hundred-pound Texas Longhorn was released and streaked away as if intending to run all the way back to Mexico. At the drop of the timer's flag, the grey pony dashed away at unbelievable speed and quickly overtook the longhorn. Mullins dropped his lariat expertly over the steer's head and Dandy turned sharply to throw the steer on its side. Finally, with Dandy holding the rope tight, Mullins was on the ground tying three legs together. He completed the test with the best time of the day. Mullins collected on the bet and a horseman came out of the crowd of spectators, wanting to buy Dandy; he would pay $750 for the little seventeen-year-old. But Dandy was not for sale, certainly not. He had a date to keep with his predecessor, the nineteen-year-old Prince, on the good grass at Weadick's ranch in the Canadian foothills.

Except for visitors who wanted pictures of themselves standing with Dandy, and distinguished guests like Edward, Prince of Wales, who called in 1923 to inspect and greet the two old horses, they enjoyed perfect peace and lots of grass and good water. Dandy lived to the age of thirty and Prince a little longer.

If horses have memories, few had more to remember than the little grey that was born Mexican, then became an American, and finally a Canadian. He had seen war service in the Mexican cavalry, and then had successive stints in wild west shows, rodeo, and vaudeville. Finally, his well-earned retirement brought him more than a decade of freedom with good care, good grass, and affection in the Canadian foothills.

Grant MacEwan

Author, environmentalist, educator, agricultural scientist, journalist, farmer and politician, Grant MacEwan is one of western Canada's most respected and prominent personalities.

From 1946 to 1951, Grant MacEwan was Dean of Agriculture at the University of Manitoba. After terms as a Calgary alderman and an Alberta MLA, he became mayor of Calgary in 1963 and in 1965 was appointed Lieutenant-Governor of Alberta, serving until 1974. He holds honorary degrees from the Universities of Alberta, Calgary, Brandon, Guelph and Saskatchewan, and is an honorary chief of the Blood Reserve.

Grant MacEwan has a total of forty-eight titles to his name—an impressive tribute to the prairies and a heart-felt celebration of the land and the people that shaped it. He now resides in Calgary, close to the hills he cherishes.